Authority, Leadership and Concern

Roger C. Wilson
Swarthmore Lecture 1949

ROGER WILSON was born in 1906 and educated at Manchester Grammar School and Queen's College, Oxford. At Oxford he was President of the Union and took First Class Honours in Philosophy, Politics and Economics in 1929. From 1929–34 he was employed in the cotton industry, and was then on the staff of the British Broadcasting Corporation until 1940, when he was dismissed as a Conscientious Objector. From 1940–46 he was General Secretary and Travelling Commissioner of the Friends Relief Service, and was then Head of the Department of Social Studies at the University College of Hull for five years. In 1951 he was a Professor of Education at the University of Bristol, with frequent leaves of absence for services overseas attached to the Pakistan Planning Board in 1955 and 1956, from 1957 on a number of occasions in Africa (particularly as a member of the United Nations Operation in the Congo, 1961–62, and the University of Malawi, 1966), and in 1964 as a Consultant in the Gilbert and Ellice Islands Colony in the Western Pacific. He served as Chairman of the Friends Service Council, 1954–61. With Margery Wilson he was a visiting member of the Quaker United Nations Programme in New York in 1951 and 1963. For twelve years he was a Justice of the Peace in Bristol, and was Chairman of the Visiting Magistrates at Shepton Mallet Prison. In 1968 he was a Visiting Professor in the Harvard University Graduate School of Education. Roger Wilson died in 1991.

Authority, Leadership and Concern

A study in motive and administration in Quaker relief work

Roger C. Wilson
Swarthmore Lecture 1949

QUAKERbooks

First published 1949 by George Allen & Unwin Ltd. who gratefully
acknowledge permission received from publishers or authors, or their
representatives, for the use of extracts reproduced in the lecture.
Pamphlet edition 1970 Friends Home Service Committee.
The pamphlet edition of the 1949 Swarthmore Lecture was reprinted for
reasons of economy without alteration to the original text.
Reprinted June 2007

PUBLISHER'S NOTE: For this reprint we have not updated the text
e.g. for changes in Quaker organisation, or references to *Christian Faith
& Practice* rather than the 1995 *Quaker Faith & Practice.*

ISBN 978 0 901689 85 6

Cover photograph: Friends Relief Service in Perpignan, France (Library
of the Religious Society of Friends, London)
Cover design: Hoop Associates
Additional typesetting: Compositions by Carn

The Swarthmore Lecture

The Swarthmore Lectureship was established by the Woodbrooke Extension Committee at a meeting held on 9 December 1907: the minute of the Committee providing for an "annual lecture on some subject relating to the message and work of the Society of Friends". The name Swarthmore was chosen in memory of the home of Margaret Fox, which was always open to the earnest seeker after Truth, and from which loving words of sympathy and substantial material help were sent to fellow workers.

The Lectureship continues to be under the care of Woodbrooke Quaker Study Centre Trustees, and is a significant part of the education work undertaken at and from Woodbrooke.

The Lectureship has a twofold purpose: first, to interpret to the members of the Society of Friends their message and mission; and second, to bring before the public the spirit, aims and fundamental principles of Friends. The lecturers alone are responsible for any opinions expressed.

The Lectureship provides both for the publication of a book and for the delivery of a lecture, the latter usually at the time of Britain Yearly Meeting of the Religious Society of Friends (London Yearly Meeting up to 1994). The lecture relating to this book was given at Friends House, London, on the evening of 20 May 1949.

The Swarthmore Lecture Committee can be contacted via the Clerk, c/o Woodbrooke Quaker Study Centre, 1046 Bristol Road, Selly Oak, Birmingham B29 6LJ.

Woodbrooke
Quaker Study Centre

Contents

FOREWORD TO PAMPHLET EDITION

During the twenty-one years since this essay was written, I have worked in four universities; as a member of an international team in Pakistan, and as a member of the United Nations Operation in the Congo. In none of these settings was there any considerable number of colleagues with religious convictions; yet in each of the settings it was possible to discern large elements of the working principles that underlay the activities of Friends Relief Service. There is no incongruity here. As Archbishop William Temple says, in the quotation on page 73, this is God's world and he reigns, whatever we believe.

The sort of organizations in which I have worked have not been untroubled by sometimes fiercely competitive interest in pay and status; nor have they been unaffected by internal struggles for personal or group power. But competition for material reward or power has been neither the starting point nor the end of our transactions with each other or the world. What has bound us together in the end has been some common concern of the spirit for moral purposes beyond any personal reward. The present restlessness in universities and schools is symptomatic of our failure to find adequate answers to mutual relationships in this sort of activity; but it is clear that the issues are about ends and relationships and not about money as the dominant criterion.

But those of us who work in settings of this kind need to remember that we are sustained economically by those who work in agriculture, industry and commerce. And it seems to me that in these fields of activity it is much more difficult to relate moral purpose and the conflicting strands in human nature in such a way as to recognise that God reigns. Competitive commitment to the acquisition of visible possessions as such has become so embedded in our economic institutions that there is very little room to assert the reality of other aspects of human motivation; it may indeed be that the world's economic single-mindedness will prove ultimately self-destructive.

For those of us who live off the economy without being totally of it, this is a disquieting line of thought. On the one hand, how do we stand in relation to world poverty if possessions are not multiplied? On the other, how do we share our partial discoveries about relationships in non-competitive employment without being smug or patronising? I do not know the answer, beyond being sure that for those of us who are in occupations that allow room for experimental growth in patterns of relationships there can be no complacency. We must try to do better in the conviction that in any dialogue between ourselves and our fellows in other occupations, insight may grow and truth be discovered.

March, 1970

FOREWORD

It is perhaps curious but none the less healthy, that, with the
exception of a short study* by Henri van Etten, there has
been almost no analysis of the principles of Quaker relief
work over the last hundred years. The work has been done
simply because Friends have felt it laid upon them to do it.
While the operations were taking place, attention was con-
centrated on the job in hand, and when that was done, those
doing it packed up and went back to their business or teaching,
or housekeeping, and were quickly much too immersed in the
next thing to have time to ruminate. The work has been
taken for granted, and has had the strengths and weaknesses
of things that have come quite spontaneously.

The unreflective origin of Quaker relief work puts it in the
reputable company of most basic human action. Men ate
before they thought about the nature of eating ; men wor-
shipped before they thought about the nature of God. And
though we may eat more wisely for some knowledge of the
principles of nutrition, and worship more reverently for some
knowledge of the workings of God, yet we should do neither
of these things but for the basic experience of eating and
worshipping, which come not from thought but from the very
nature of life itself. No amount of theorizing about artistic
creation would turn a man who could not paint, into an
artist. So no amount of thinking about relief work will make a
good relief worker or a good relief organization.

The following essay looks at Quaker relief work with an
analytic eye, not because I believe it can be explained, but
because experience in it helped many of us to know something
more of the will and ways of God in his dealings with men,
than any other experience in our lives. My conclusion will
not be that Truth is to be found and captured by adopting

* " Ouriers avec Dieu," transl. into English in *Friends Quarterly Examiner*,
April, 1946.

this trick or that, by applying this formula or that procedure, or even that a Friends Yearly Meeting is always right. It will be that there is a way of living which is of God, which does not abolish or even diminish conflicts, perplexities, failures, but which does enable these to be overcome as we have faith in His strength. This is no new discovery except for ourselves. Like our predecessors in Friends' relief work, 1914-1923, " Our experiences have made many of us know the great truths of religion with a certainty not reached before."*

One warning must be plainly uttered. Inevitably in examining the nature of action which we believe to be right, emphasis tends to be laid upon the best elements in the action. And so an idealized picture of action is liable to be built up. In the Friends Relief Service, 1940-48, there was much faithfulness and some heroism, especially by some of those who did lonely jobs in remote places, but most of us who were involved were very much aware of the frequent shoddiness of actual performance due partly to incompetence, and partly to the weakness of our spirit of Charity. Just as Christianity is continuously defiled by the weakness of men, so the Christian quality of our Quaker service was continuously weakened by the poverty of our living. Our action and our principles were always coming adrift. This lecture is about principles.

* A. Ruth Fry, *A Quaker Adventure*, p. xx.

AUTHORITY, LEADERSHIP AND CONCERN

QUAKER RELIEF WORK

" We were to meet in the Rathaus, a red-bricked building in an undamaged suburb of the town. The warm smell of the wall-flowers outside lingered as we passed through the swing doors, to be defeated by the familiar smell of municipal offices (the same in Salford or Solingen) which hung about the corridors.

We went up the stone staircase with its walls of shabby green paint to the council chamber on the first floor. On the far side of the long oval table sat nineteen German Fursorgerinnen, with the Stadtrat, an old man with white hair and whiskers, in the arm-chair at the head. He shook hands with our team leader and offered her a chair on his right. We followed and took the empty places opposite, eleven of us in Quaker grey.

I looked around at the leather-covered table with its heavy glass ink-stands, the portraits of deceased notabilities, the Turkey carpet, the high windows and the moulded ceiling. We might have been in Manchester, except that the Stadtrat was talking in German. We knew something of his history, he had lost his office and gone into retirement in 1933, and now, although over seventy, had returned to serve his native town. It was evidently a formal speech of welcome he was making. . . . The Stadtrat's eloquence ended at last. It was our turn. M. spoke for us. This was no set speech, and the atmosphere quickened. The German women leaned forward a little, all eyes were turned on her. She spoke briefly of the Quakers, of their origin and history ; of the Friends Relief Service, of its work among war-victims in the occupied countries ; of our own team's arrival in Germany a week ago.

' We want to help where we can, and we hope you will tell us how. That is why we want to work with you and go with you on your rounds next week. And our motive ? ' She paused, and in that second's pause flicked through my mind the realization that we were foreigners, British, part and yet not part of the conquering, occupying force. Would they let us help ? Would they accept us ? Could we do any good ? 'And our motive ? Just the Christian one, the motive of the good Samaritan.' "

That is a rather more dramatic picture of the beginning of relief operation than usual. But in essence it tells the story of the beginning of almost any of the relief jobs done by the Friends Relief Service during and after the second world war, whether it was the establishment of a hostel for elderly air-raid victims in Ulster or Suffolk, the establishment of a residential rural economy school for village girls in Macedonia, the making of toys in Regent's Park for war nurseries, the conducting of evacuation surveys in Plymouth, the feeding of orphans in Poland, the running of a provincial transport service in Normandy, the treating of scabies in Holland, the visiting of prisons in Germany, the collection of the vine harvest in the Aegean island of Samos, the making habitable of hopfield barracks in Herefordshire, or the organization of welfare services under the railway arch refuges of Stepney—or any other of the varied situations in which we found ourselves involved. Most of these jobs began quite naturally and simply by people doing what seemed to them to be the obviously right thing to do next in the place where they found themselves.

But if we look more closely into the chain of events leading up to these operations, the simplicity disappears. How did people able to do these and similar things come to be in Palestine and East Africa, Ireland, the Yorkshire Wolds, Gibraltar, Vienna, the Potteries or Bethnal Green? And that leads on to enquiry about the origin of the tradition of relief work which has been built up around the Society of Friends, often to its embarrassment when those in distress have assumed that Quakers could do anything and have discovered that they have as many limitations as the next organization; often to the injustice of other groups doing first-rate relief work and assumed, *ipso facto*, but quite unfairly, to be Quakers. Actually, the amount of relief work done by Quakers is small compared with that done by many other organizations; the fact remains that a tradition has been built up and that it does rest on substantial foundations.

In the first two and a half centuries of the Society's existence, there was much private philanthropy, and quite a deal of organized corporate effort, even if the machinery was rudimentary and somewhat unofficial by present standards.

2

There were elements of relief work in seventeenth and eighteenth century efforts to deal with unemployment. In the American War of Independence, Philadelphia Friends took succour to Friends in Boston which was beseiged by the British. British Friends raised money for the relief of distress following a Turkish massacre of Greek Christians in the Island of Chios in 1823. But probably the first occasion on which Friends both raised money from the general public and appointed an official committee of some of their own number actually to administer the relief service in the field was during the Irish Famine of 1846, when Dublin Yearly Meeting raised funds, with the help of Friends in Britain and America, for constructive use in the West of Ireland.*

The work of the four successive Friends War Victims Relief Committees in France, the Balkans, Russia, Central and Western Europe between 1870 and 1923 is more familia.. In the absence of such *ad hoc* committees the Friends Service Council and its ancestral forerunners have often taken a hand in relief work of one sort and another, overseas or among refugees and interned people in this country. Here at home, the Coalfields Distress Committee and its descendant, the Friends Allotments Committee, have done a job among the unemployed and the aged since 1926 that has had some significant social and economic consequences. The American Friends Service Committee has rendered service in its own country and overseas in a very wide range of social disasters and tense human situations. The small groups of Quakers on the European continent have frequently come to the rescue of their fellow-citizens or of their national enemies who have been in great need. These are examples, mentioned not for the glorification of the Quaker name in its relief context, but showing that organized relief effort by Friends has some substantial roots.

* See the admirable critical account of its own work published by the Committee in 1852 : Transactions of the Central Relief Committee of the Society of Friends during Famine in Ireland in 1846-47.

CONCERN

" . . . the Living Christ within us is the initiator and we are the responders. God, the lover, the accuser, the revealer of light and darkness presses within us. ' Behold I stand at the door and knock.' And all our apparent initiative is already a response, a testimonial to His secret presence and working within us."

" A concern is God-initiated, often surprising, always holy, for the Life of God is breaking through into the world. Its execution is in peace and power and astounding faith and joy, for in unhurried security the Eternal is at work in the midst of time, triumphantly bringing all things up unto Himself." Thomas Kelly. *A Testament of Devotion.*

If a Quaker relief group were suddenly asked to explain themselves they would probably be nearly inarticulate at first and might then manage to express themselves in the sense of the concluding words of the report with which the previous section began—" Our motive ? Just the Christian one, the motive of the Good Samaritan." It sounds simple enough ; it represents a compelling experience familiar to millions of men, of whom only a tiny fraction have been Quakers, who have gone out of their way to give help to friends and enemies. But in any analytical sense, it begs substantial questions, about three of which I wish to say something.

To begin with, the Good Samaritan was not a Christian ; so what do we mean if we say that his motive was a Christian one ? Secondly, the impulse to help people in distress does not, of itself, dig people out of their jobs and homes and send them off looking for trouble on an organized basis. And thirdly, a common impulse may be the origin of organized service, but the organization itself is a very complex thing, and so far as Quaker relief work in the nineteen-forties is concerned, it was an organization bearing little resemblance to any organization with which most of us are familiar in our working lives.

4

THE GOOD SAMARITAN

The Good Samaritan was not a Christian. He was a Jew from Samaria. The orthodox Jews regarded Samaritans as misguided deviationists from the Jewish tradition, and in Samaria, Jesus was himself not well received. It was not from the Samaritan tradition that Christianity was born, and yet we Christians have come to claim the Good Samaritan as the very pattern of Christian conduct. It is a curious arrogance which leads us to appropriate as specifically Christian a virtue whose best known expression is attributed by Jesus himself to a non-Christian outsider. Plainly what moved the Samaritan was a spiritual experience which is prior to the structure and theology which have been built on the experience of those who knew and were taught by Jesus and who followed him.

Relief work then, which claims kinship with that of the Good Samaritan, is something which springs from an experience which, in itself, can be known independently of the framework of the Christian Church as it has developed since the days of Jesus. It goes back to roots in the nature of the universe, which is, perhaps, a pompous way of saying that simple human kindness, expressed at some personal cost, is a natural quality in man. In so far as anybody is motivated by it, there is nothing that differentiates Christians in general, let alone Quakers in particular, from Jews, Mohammedans, Hindus, or atheists.

What is, I think, peculiar to Christianity is its refusal to regard with cynicism the fact that alongside this capacity sometimes to behave like the Samaritan there goes a capacity for frequently behaving like the Priest and the Levite. Our failures do not cut us off from the pursuing Love of God. Instead of going from bad to worse, at the speed which our human failures would justify, we are, by the Grace of God, continually rescued from ourselves; it is a quite extraordinarily logical mind which is able to pursue a consistent policy of neglect of other men and which never lapses into generosity. Christianity builds on both men's capacity for self-forgetfulness and on their capacity for failure, so that they

5

can set out on an effort to serve their fellows, well knowing that they will often stumble, but equally certain that God will draw them forwards, granting them strength, courage, repentance, and spirit to go on. Christians can build on their failures. They can live and serve in a world of priests, Levites, and Good Samaritans, without being overwhelmed by its evil or sentimentally optimistic about its goodness. They need not be saints before they set out deliberately to serve their neighbours, not incidentally, but, if one may put it so without misunderstanding, professionally.

PACIFIST SERVICE IN WAR-TIME

And so we come to our second question ; what is it that picked us up out of our settled ways all over the country, and put us together into an organization which then dumped us down in scores of scattered locations extending over thousand of miles, where we were able in some small way to give help to people in distress ?

The superficial answer is that most of us were conscientious objectors whose ordinary way of life was closed to us either because we had been dismissed from our jobs, or because our jobs had come to an end, or because the Tribunals had obliged us to leave our jobs, or because, of our own free will, we had left our peacetime jobs to join the Friends Relief Service. Without the influence of conscription, few of us would, perhaps, have left peacetime work which for some, if not for all, of us was a vocation. But that is not by any means the whole story. The British Government and people were generous to conscientious objectors in the second world war, and almost any of us could, without much difficulty, have obtained civilian work in agriculture, food production, education, hospitals and so on, which would not have outraged our conscientious objections to participation in war. Many pacifists, in fact, did this ; just as others deliberately went to gaol as their testimony in a society whose primary purpose was the prosecution of the war.

What processes were at work that made us join the Relief

Service rather than respond in any other way to the war situation ? The question itself divides into four parts. Why should individuals devote themselves to relief work rather than, say, hospital service ? Why should they attach themselves to the relief service of the Society of Friends ? Why should the Society of Friends take responsibility anyway for running a sizeable relief organization ? Why should the Society of Friends accept the offers of service of many who were not its members, and reject the offers of many who were ?

MOTIVES

1. Motives were, as always, very mixed. Some of us were moved in part by a straight desire for something of the adventure which is possible in wartime, in pacifist organizations as in war-like ones. Some of us wanted to find out if our pacifism had any link with physical cowardice, and went looking for danger. Others of us, without looking exactly for adventure, saw in relief work a chance to do something more interesting than had come our way as bank clerks, or shorthand typists and the like. Some of us were acutely aware of our material privileges in peace-time society and we thought that life in the Relief Service would introduce us to a simplicity of living which would set our minds at peace. (Life in the Service was fairly simple for the most part. But the amount of hardship, as distinct from frustration and boredom, was not great ; and it was probably wives and families who carried the main burden of drab financial stringency, unrelieved by the stimulus of group life and the intermittent movement within the Service itself.) Some of us looked forward to work whose effects in human life were obvious and immediate.

Then there were the by no means inconsiderable number seeking an escape from worries of their own of one sort or another. It might be that they were looking for some respectable reason for leaving home ; more frequently it was their hope that in some form of constructive work they would find release from frustration of the spirit that dogged them in everyday life. I well remember several talks with one of the most deeply passionate writers of this generation who felt utterly sick of trying to make satisfying sense of the world by any sort of verbal or intellectual process, and who felt that in working among misery with Friends, he might find peace of soul. This attitude is, of course, very prevalent among many philanthropists. Much good work has its roots in this hunger of the spirit.

I remember talking with a member of the Service on an Aegean Island where the work was largely concerned with rather miserable refugees and the problems of settling them back, after years of purposeless demoralization in refugee camps, into the places from which they had originally come. He had been working alongside relief workers in secular agencies, and what had impressed him was the inability of the secular workers to stand up to the sheer misery of the situation. They had come out with high ideals about the way in which society should be organized and about the part they could play. They had come out with romantic views about the way in which needy people would respond to good, sensible leading. And they had found themselves engulfed by human wreckage, by people who were wretched, dirty, quarrelsome, liars, thieves, stupid in big issues, astutely selfish in little ones, just about as unpromising a lot of citizens for the new Jerusalem as could populate the worst nightmares. In such a situation, the secular reformer and lover of his fellows found no field of service. No noticeable results could possibly follow his efforts, persistence in which led merely to failure and cyncism. Nothing, said my colleague, save Christian love could serve in that situation to keep the relief worker sane, and to him and his fellow-workers there had come a hitherto unappreciated vitality in the Christian teaching about the way in which men are bound to one another for no other reason than their common membership in the family of God.

This attitude was not one that was met much in those who had not yet done relief work. It was an understanding that grew on the field—in evacuation hostels at home, no less than in work abroad. What weighed, perhaps, more among those contemplating service, was the position of the Christian pacifist in the community. For many sensitive Christian pacifists there was no obvious clear-cut course in world war as experienced by us in this country in 1939-1945. Our conviction that all war is wrong is not based on a conviction of the absence of evil in men, though some pacifists do seem to slip into this error.

Christian pacifism is based on an assertion that alongside man's immense capacity for sin and evil there is an eternal capacity for goodness and the things of God, and that it is only as this capacity for goodness is continually called to express itself that men, both callers and called, escape from the bonds of evil. Assertion of the supremacy of the claims of goodness over evil does not naturally make for safety or success as usually understood. The Crucifixion is a typical example of what happens when loyalty to the things of God is pursued to the end. Now, in the war, I do not think that any of us could doubt the colossal quality of the evil represented by Nazi philosophy. And I do not think that, in political terms, it was possible to contemplate coming to any sort of political compromise with it. Political peace negotiations with Hitler were morally, no less than diplomatically, impossible. Speaking personally as a Christian pacifist, I had a far deeper sense of spiritual unity with those of my friends in the fighting services, who, detesting war as deeply as I did, yet felt that there was no other way in which they could share in the agony of the world, than I had with those pacifists who talked as if the suffering of the world could be turned off like a water tap if only politicians would talk sensibly together. Where men have sinned as grievously and as long as we have done in our social and international relations with one another, there can be no easy end to the consequences. The wages of sin is death, and nothing can stop the wages being collected except the readiness shared by some pacifists and some belligerents to suffer redemptively, which is one of the paradoxically healing ways of God. In a war situation, I do not believe that we Christian pacifists have much to say on a political level, since we cannot accept the presuppositions regarding power which are so preponderant in a world at war. I believe that our obligation is :

> To love and bear : to hope till hope creates
> From its own wreck the thing it contemplates.

We could not engage in warlike activity in the hope of relieving the suffering of the Jews or of other oppressed peoples in Europe and Asia. We had, somehow, to try to participate in their suffering and to express the conviction that it is ultimately the power of suffering in love that redeems men from the power of evil. Few of us felt entirely confident that our love and imagination were of such a quality as to justify the practice of our convictions about our answer to the suffering of our oppressed fellows, especially when we remembered that many of our free fellow-countrymen were fighting and dying, amongst other reasons, for our right as pacifists to practise this conviction. And yet, for all our unclarity, we were clear that God would not have us fight. In this state of mind, many of us found ourselves drawn towards relief work with a conviction amounting to concern that this was the way God would have us respond to the failures and possibilities in which we were living.

QUAKER SERVICE

2. In contemplating relief work at home and abroad some of us found Friends Relief Service the natural body to which to attempt to attach ourselves. We were Friends ; we felt conscientiously unable to attach ourselves to the unofficial but very enterprising Friends Ambulance Unit because we could not accept its " alternative service " basis or its requirement that we should be willing to undertake army ambulance work if required ; or, while we had no conscientious difficulty in accepting the basis of the Unit, we had financial obligations for dependants for which the terms of Unit membership did not provide but for which Friends Relief Service could. Many who were not Friends probably offered their services in the first instance for no other reason than that Friends had,

rightly or wrongly, a good reputation as a relief agency. But others felt drawn to an organization with a specifically religious basis. Some, while not personal pacifists in relation to the war itself, yet felt that personal and social relationships could best be expressed, so far as they were concerned, through relief work in an organization trying to implement Christian pacifist convictions. As one considered offers of service and talked with those who made them, one realized what a wide range of personal outlooks seemed to focus themselves on the possibilities of the Society of Friends. Quakers must do much disciplined thinking about their responsibilities to hungry sheep who are not fed and who think that there may be something for them in the Quaker fold. A pure-bred pedigree flock looks well ; and it feels good to be a member. But imaginative cross-breeding may be what is required of us. I am not sure that we were as bold as we might well have been in accepting offers of service from people who were far from clear why they wanted to work with Friends, but who were quite clear that they wanted to work with us.

CORPORATE QUAKER CONCERN

3. But why should the Society involve itself in large-scale relief work at all ?

Many people outside the Society and some within regard it as primarily a social work agency, specializing in emergency relief overseas. Why this should be so is puzzling, for in Great Britain the Society has no standing machinery for doing relief work. When the fifth Friends War Victims Relief Committee* since 1870 was appointed in the autumn of 1940, perhaps half a dozen of its members had had sporadic experience of relief work in the field during the first world war and its aftermath or in the European civil wars ; and the presence of these Friends on the 1940 Committee maintained the tradition. But from start to finish, only one member of the central or field administration had had any previous experience of relief work, and of the actual field workers, not more

* The name was changed to Friends Relief Service in 1943.

than about a score out of a total of something over 1,000 had previously worn the Quaker service star.

The Society is not a relief organization. It is a branch of the Christian Church, with the same essential functions as any other branch of the Christian Church—the worship of God and the bringing of men to His footstool. In the light of its Christian experience, the Society has certain " testimonies " to proclaim about the nature of human relationships under the authority of God ; it believes that the teaching of Jesus refers to the conduct of men as they earn their livings and have dealings with their fellows near and far. It has always believed that God speaks to men directly, that the " Light of Christ " can illumine each individual soul, that there is no need for the professional service of priests, which can indeed be deadening to the Christian experience and responsibility of every man, and that little but danger lurks in the authority of an ordained hierarchy. Given this background to their corporate Church life, members of the Society of Friends have naturally come to have a high regard for the mutual responsibilities of citizenship. While, therefore, the primary purpose of the Society is Worship, with its emphasis on *being*, as the underlying experience from which right *doing* naturally follows, there are occasions on which corporate *doing* is laid upon members as a result of a sense of " concern " developing through corporate and mutually dependant Worship of God.

" Concern " is a word which has tended to become debased by excessively common usage among Friends, so that too often it is used to cover merely a strong desire. The true " concern " is a gift from God, a leading of his Spirit which may not be denied. Its sanction is not that on investigation it proves an intelligent thing to do—though it usually is ; it is that the individual, and if his concern is shared and adopted by the Meeting, then the Meeting knows, as a matter of inward experience, that here is something which the Lord would have done, however obscure the way, however uncertain the means to human observation. Often proposals for action are made which have every appearance of good sense, but as the meeting waits before God, it becomes clear that the proposition falls short of " concern."

The latter part of this lecture is very largely about the relation between the inspiration of " concern " and sound sense when a Quaker organization starting from a " concern " is embarked on an enterprise where decisions have to be taken before inspiration is forthcoming. For the moment it is enough to emphasize that corporate action in the Society is rooted in Worship and not in debate or philosophical analysis or social synthesis. When Friends have established a relief organization, it has been the result of a sense of " concern."*

But it is unlikely that a "concern" emerges from blank minds or empty spirits, however humbly they wait. I believe there are good predisposing reasons why, in face of a major social disaster like war or mass unemployment, the Society of Friends may well have things on its conscience which lead it to think in terms of corporate action and to find that it has a " concern."

The worst human disasters are rarely " acts of God.'' Just as wars and persecution, unemployment and poverty, are the results of the failure of society as a whole to bear its responsibilities, so famine often has its roots in the same failure. From the immediate consequences of these failures, Friends have been largely immune for two deep reasons. On the one hand, they tend not to find themselves among the economically insecure. This is less of a reproach than is sometimes thought ; for any Christian group which takes its religious life seriously is likely to display through the lives of its members a high degree of industry, sobriety, educational responsibility and integrity ; and they need not lack grace and humour, though too often they do. Given these qualities in the family, lowliness in this world's estate in one generation is not likely to persist in the next. When social disaster overtakes the poor, Friends as a whole, tend to remain immune. In the second place, in so far as war is concerned, most Friends in

* For a valuable discussion of the relationship between individual and corporate concern see " Quaker Service," Edward Milligan, *Friends Quarterly*, April, 1948.

the English-speaking world tend to remain relatively immune
from personal and family danger because of their pacifism.
Conscription may be an anxiety and burden for some, but for
most of us, who think that the job we do in peace is the right
thing to continue to do in war-time, war is a cloud over the
whole of our lives rather than an acute crisis, as it is for the
majority of homes with members of one or more generations
away fighting. It is for these reasons that we ourselves tend
to remain sheltered from the disasters that befall our fellows,
not for their personal failings, but as the result of the failings of
all of us.

It is here that I believe we may find some explanation of
the corporate concern of the Society to respond in an emergency. Whether we are intellectually aware of the social
nature of the failing or not, there is, at time like these, an
unusually acute sense of the unity of God's creation. The
fact that honesty pays, the fact that our pacifism preserves us
from a sense of obligation to do some things that many who do
them profoundly detest—these are no good reasons, at times
of exceptional disaster to stand apart from the misery, the
boredom, possibly the physical danger, of famine and war.
In one way or another we must try to offer our bodies a living
sacrifice.

In some measure this should be a continuing sense of
responsibility in a Christian society ; and I venture to think
that it is not entirely absent from among us. While it seems
to me inevitable that a Christian society should tend to find
itself accumulating property or respect or both, it also seems
to me to follow that neither it nor its members should become
inextricably wealthy or respectable. There comes a point at
which like lesser Woolmans, Friends will turn from excessive
interest in their professional occupations in order to serve in
less economic ways ; there comes a point at which personal
wealth is not spent personally ; there comes a point at which
the Society corporately—though unconsciously—tends to
turn from economic activity altogether and to devote itself to
the non-material tasks of teaching and preaching and serving.
There *is* a vicarious balance within society and within our

Society whereby some turn directly to the service of others, while some stay in difficult economic or moral situations presented by contemporary society. Membership one of another is a very real thing, even when we are quite unaware of it. This is not, in itself, surprising if we think of the implications of our faith—that this is God's world ; that we are finite and fallible creatures, but that God is always taking the initiative by his Grace, making us better than we appear to be, so that we are able at times of inspiration to support one another in ways we do not understand.

It is in terms like these that we may see how a corporate concern can take hold of our Society and how the continuous concern is related to the concern to do something more in a crisis. At all times in a sensitive and united social group there will be an awareness that its integration imposes on it the necessity to try to minister to the disintegration of the larger society ; at special moments of human failure, the smaller group will feel that the crisis of disintegration must be answered by special service. Hence the establishment of intermittent relief committees.

4. In considering how relief workers are selected, there are two issues.

What is relief work ; and what sort of people are needed to do it ?

THE NATURE OF RELIEF WORK

Most relief work begins with some obvious physical need. But almost always there is, behind the physical need, something much less concrete, a damaged or lonely or hopeless or hungry spirit, and relief work which does not penetrate to this level, directly or indirectly, consciously or unconsciously, and make some contribution to healing is a job only partially done. This is not to say that physical relief is not worth doing, and the unconscious and indirect effects of it may be of great constructive significance. For instance, the mere arrival and continued presence of substantial numbers of young men and women of the F.A.U. in Stepney air-raid shelters in 1940-41 brought in an element of courage and resourcefulness to reinforce those locally responsible, although the young men and women themselves had for the most part very little idea of what they were doing beyond a necessary physical job. Given a little outside help of this kind, the local inhabitants and officials were quite capable of regaining and maintaining their power to cope with circumstances at first overwhelming. Or again, the mere presence in Normandy of a transport unit, willing and able to undertake the carriage of socially necessary materials in the early chaotic days of rebuilding, probably did a good job in saving many from the cynicism that followed in the track of otherwise almost universal black-market transport practices. Spirits can be broken by sheer physical exhaustion and to relieve the crushing pressure may be a spiritual ministry of a high order.

At the other end of the types of relief work stands a recollection of a visit to France in the late autumn of 1944 in the company of a veteran Quaker relief and social worker, who had rendered much service in France during the first world war, and subsequently between the wars. We were probably among the first civilian relief workers to have reached France from outside after the Liberation, and we found the French organizations engaged in coping with their own enormous problems and grappling with the most terrible difficulties—broken communications, shortage of supplies of every kind, personnel shortages, chronically unheated offices and homes, undermanned, demoralized and disorganized public services and what not. The will was there, but it was engulfed in the lonely hopelessness of a country only just freed from German occupation and still regarded primarily by the dominant American and British military as a base for warlike operations. But the transformation when my veteran colleague walked unexpectedly into an office of old French friends ! One saw the change on their faces from fear of defeat to courage and hope and confidence, and as she talked with them, one realized what an amazing effect could follow from the simple introduction of the appropriate personality into situations. For at that time we had neither personnel nor supplies to offer to the French. We had nothing save our interest to put at their disposal—and the affection and deep understanding of my elderly colleague for French people and French needs. To me it threw quite new light on the parable of the loaves and fishes. For here was a living, current example of how the very limited resources of the French organizations could be stretched beyond belief, simply by the presence of a visitor who brought qualities of the spirit for which the liberated French were hungry.

Here is another instance. It is the end of the account that I quoted earlier about the introduction of the relief team to the local welfare workers in a Ruhr town.

" Three weeks later I sat in the translucent green of a late May evening, on the banks of the River Wupper, and heard from the ' Fursorgerin ' with whom I had worked something of what that Saturday morning had meant to her and her colleagues on the other side of the table. She was thirty-two and a devout Catholic. In 1933 she had been a girl at College. What the gathering darkness and horror of the Nazi regime had meant to her I was able to guess as much from her reticence as her disclosures. I could guess at the confusion of mind of one whose only source of information was the official news service, but whose principles were rooted in the gospel that there is neither bond nor free, Jew nor Greek.

Then came the collapse of Germany : and like so many others C. awoke to find that isolation was followed not by liberation but by ostracism. The world had rung with the horrors of Belsen and Buchenwald ; and shame, despair, resentment and wounded pride had produced a condition of complete negativism.

Complete ? Not quite. These people we had met were ' Fursorgerinnen.' The name means ' those who care for.' They might have neither hope nor political philosophy, but they had a job to do. On each of these welfare workers depended some thousands of people, the poorest and most helpless, the old, the needy, the babies. And so, in the deepening want of post-war Germany, they took up the burden of their vocation with a courage and an integrity that commands our respect.

When their head ' Fursorgerin ' summoned them to meet the English Quakers at nine o'clock that Saturday in May, they had but the vaguest idea of what they would find. Another branch of Military Government perhaps ? Some of the older ones remembered Quaker feeding after the last war ; all of them recalled that school feeding introduced by Military Government had—for some reason—spontaneously been dubbed ' Quakerspeisung.'

What they did find was a company of amateurs with no claims to superior knowledge and no axe to grind. They resorted to metaphor in their attempt to make us realize what our coming meant to them ; a breath of fresh wind ; a door opened on to the world after years of imprisonment. It can all be summed up quite simply ; they found that *someone* cared.

'We have been trying to help others and to give them courage out of our own bankruptcy,' said C. 'We have gone on in despair, feeling that our country is an outcast from civilized society, that everyone hates us, and that we have no future. It is not merely the material aid you bring, though we need it desperately. You can imagine what it is for a " Fursorgerin " to be empty-handed when she is asked for help. But since you came I have wakened each morning without a load on my heart.'

Across the river the shadows of the trees grew longer. We sat on a while in silence, willing to postpone the moment when we must pick up our bicycles and return to the half-bombed town.

'I was anhungered and ye fed me . . . naked and ye clothed me.' Thus would most people epitomize the purpose of relief work. But in ruined and outcast Germany the words that came alive again, at least for me, were ' . . . in prison, and ye came unto me.' "

But whether the first approach is on the level of supplies or sustenance for the spirit, these things cannot fulfil their real purpose unless offered by each individual in a creative spirit. Remember that this work was being done in the midst of total war or its aftermath. You and I and the people in distress were all both responsible for, and part of, the processes of destruction in the middle of which we were living. And the best Quaker relief work has, I think, sprung from a sense of common sin, leading to a sense of common repentance. This is not emotional regret but a real intention to break into the circle of sin and suffering by living in the grace of God whose will for us in any particular situation is a real objective fact which can be known through prayer and worship, and which is not merely a device or an expedient or a compromise. Inspired relief workers cease to be external agents ; like Woolman they have a sense of " being mixed in with " suffering mankind : unselfconsciously they become part of the chaos, the misery and the perplexity in which they move, and yet they neither accept nor are degraded by the situation. Because of their certainity of the Will of God for them they are not frightened to find themselves in the centre of the world's evil, and because of their experience of the love of God, they have the patience and the understanding to speak to the condition of their fellows. They do not go about looking for a job to do. They are drawn by their divinely-rooted imagination to the service of God and their fellows in the way that the Lord wills.

A relief organization, then, ought to be a corporate body capable of both common-sense and imaginative action, combined with a natural ability to convey to others a sense of inner peace and stability, surviving outward chaos and yet not divorced from it. And though it will not find many volunteers who come up to this all-round standard, it must select its members with care.

THE RELIEF WORKER

The potential raw material of a Quaker relief organization is not, at first sight, particularly promising. For most of it is available or potentially available in war-time in virtue of its pacifism and its claim to conscientious objection to military service. Now while Christian pacifists do not regard the element of " objection " as nearly so important in their whole outlook as their sense of conscientious obligation, which does not find its way into military service acts, yet most of us pacifists have more than a streak of political anarchy in our make-up. How should it be otherwise when we proclaim that there are real conflicts where the Will of God must take precedence over the law of the state or the custom of the community ? And this conviction means that most of us spend most of our lives in a critical attitude towards the society of which we are a part. We Christian pacifists are the sort of people who are usually in a minority on most of the issues arising in our schools, offices, unions, workshops or professional organizations. Pacifists as such can very easily become " minority-minded " and there is not much basis for active unity among themselves on the mere common objection to being conscripted for military or near-military purposes.

Yet our relief work depended very much upon the co-operation of individual members, for it involved a high

measure of administrative coherence, which had to be maintained without any of the usual methods of discipline—
differential rates of pay, clear grades of seniority, security or
insecurity, long periods of training or, at first, a long tradition
to which new-comers conformed by social pressure.

The large central core of the service had, therefore, to be
people at peace with God, and with themselves. These were
the people with common-sense, patience, staying-power,
humour and a capacity not to ask so many questions of
themselves and everybody else that they could never settle
down to the business of living ordinary friendly lives ; they
were very ordinary people so touched by the grace of God
that they may be said to have been divinely ordinary, neither
sentimental, nor hard, just entirely reliable and straight-
forwardly intelligent, capable of spotting anything " phoney,"
but the sort of people whom others would instinctively trust
as not being excessively clever.

The central core of ordinary people was important because
wherever there were two or more members of the service
working together, there was potential tension, which could
easily develop to intolerable limits when there was sharp
assertion of individual characteristics. In most secular
situations this tension either exists, and is ignored (when the
job is badly done), or is avoided because the relation of the
parties is purely functional and personal factors barely enter
in. But in relief work, all members were very much one of
another, all shared ultimate moral responsibility equally, and
very often there was virtually no possibility of physical private
life. If life in the working groups was therefore to be toler-
able, the majority of people had to have that natural internal
peace which could treat superficial tensions at their appropriate level. The insensitive individualist, either the one who
insisted on his rights, or, more frequently among us, the man
who always knew what was right, could only be absorbed in
very small quantities.

But while a central core of peaceful and intelligent people
was essential, this alone was not enough, for the development
of the Service depended very considerably on creative ideas

and inspirations available to the service through a minority.
Every organization needs ideas, but no organization can stand
more than a certain number at any one time, and people with
ideas are often far from easy members of groups. Without
our creative members the Service would have been inert, but
without a large body of sensible ordinary members, the
creative minds would have confused one another excessively.

The importance of a balanced environment is great, if
ideas and exceptional abilities are to be used to their best
advantage. For outstanding individuals are not by any
means always very well balanced. Imagination often resides
in those with intense inner conflicts ; drive in those who lack a
sense of personal inner security ; inspiration in those who are
careless about details ; capacity for understanding people in
those who do not mind much about administration ; administrative ability in those who think along well-set lines. Sometimes, of course, people do emerge with exceptional qualities in
the desired mixture, but ability is wasted if it cannot be used
when lop-sided. The more intelligently stable the group
temperament, the more readily can exceptional abilities find
useful and constructive scope for their expression.

Personality matters immensely in the drabness of much
relief work ; and the key to its preservation and growth, with a
strengthening, rather than a weakening, of group solidarity,
lies in the Meeting for Worship, where our individual strengths
and weaknesses are caught up in the purposes of God, so that
our contributions are made at a rich personal level while being
rooted in a common experience which is very deep.

This conception of ordinary and extraordinary personalities
being alike necessary to one another and of their building one
another up, should not be strange to Friends, for Yearly
Meeting provides an example. Probably not more than about
one-tenth of those present takes any vocal part in the deliberations ; most of the more helpful vocal contributions as well as
many of the least helpful, come from a very few members,
some of whom may contribute several times ; and some of
whom may be very awkward personalities. So far as verbal
support or dissent is concerned, the majority of members

contribute nothing except an occasional " I hope so." They do not even contribute by a silent vote. On the face of it, would not Yearly Meeting be better held by leaving matters to a few chosen delegates, capable of expressing themselves ? Our experience is that outward expressions by speech, acclamation, voting, are well avoided altogether, because they are no substitutes for the steadying experience of the group waiting quietly on the guidance of the Lord, and expressing its sense by no corporate outward or audible or visible sign.

In the Society itself, as known in our own country, the expression of " membership one of another " has worked itself out with varying quality over three centuries without much conscious effort. But in the Relief Service, we had to build a structure quickly, and we had to build it soundly enough to do a good relief job in terms of work output and also to do it in such a way that its administration and " spirit " conformed to the Quaker pattern whence it had sprung. We had, in a sense, to build a microcosm of the Society of Friends at its very best, because it was only at its best that the Service could hope to do a good enough job to carry the conviction of the Society as a whole or of its own members who had joined the Service to do a job for which they thought the Society was peculiarly well fitted.

SELECTING RELIEF WORKERS

Something like one in ten of the offers of service were accepted ; more than half of the offers from Friends were not accepted and of those people who were accepted only about two out of five were actually members of the Society. What were those who had to do the selecting looking for ?

They had, in the very first place, to look for physical health and mental robustness. Then they had, of course, to look for competence at some skill or skills that were needed. In some respects this was easy, in some difficult. It was easy, if the person had long experience or a professional qualification, to estimate what that amounted to in ordinary life. But would a good schoolmaster make a good organizer of a building squad ? Or would a nurse reared for years in well-organized

hospitals with equipment and staff at command be able to turn
to and make something of a stable, an open-air fire, a couple
of petrol tins and a candle ? Or would a competent
accountant, not needed for or even offering his services for
accountancy, be able to run an old people's evacuation
hostel ? I suppose that not one in six Quaker relief workers
was doing what he or she was trained to do. Like Dr.
Johnson's dog, the thing that astonished us was not that we
often did things badly but that we did some of them at all.

We had to fight hard against one of the well-rooted
weaknesses of Christian organization—the assumption that
provided the spirit is sound all will come well. " Good
intentions," " the right spirit," " a beautiful soul," are fine
possessions, but dangerous in relief work, unless accompanied
by a sound sense of the sort of situation in which they can be
appropriately used. Many a saint is an intolerable colleague
on a relief job and this must be recognized. Co-operative
working on practical jobs under divine guidance needs a deal
of horse-sense.

But while it was sometimes difficult to estimate competence
to do a relief job, it was always child's play as compared with
estimating motivation and its appropriateness to Christian
service under the Society of Friends, especially since it is
unfair to judge motivation in relation to verbal power to
express it, and Friends rightly reject adherence to formulæ
as of any ultimate significance.

As suggested earlier, the motives of volunteers could be very
various, and almost always they were mixed. To have mixed
motives may be the beginning of growth rather than evidence
of decay. What was much more important than an assess-
ment of the obvious motives was an effort to see how far the
volunteer understood or was likely to grow to understand
the kind of experience referred to earlier as lying at the heart
of relief work.* Good relief work cannot, in the end be done
by those who lack a sense of responsibility to and for their
fellows, based not on a desire to dominate or even to lead, but
on a conviction about the nature of the universe which may

* See p. 8 and p. 18.

23

be revealed or concealed or left quite uncertain in terms of spoken language. Given this conviction there could without damage, be quite a mixture of motivation. What mattered was that the underlying sense of responsibility should grow as experience accumulated, so that, especially in moments of crisis when action had to be taken without reflection, it should be the dominant motif.

It was also necessary to try to estimate how far the volunteer was likely to be able to feel at home in the peculiar methods of determining policy, and of allocating responsibility that are adopted by Friends. Since this theme is developed later, it is enough to say here that the Quaker tradition in government is not easily caught by those at home in other traditions with stronger hierarchical or elected elements, in which authority is placed squarely on individuals. Sometimes people who certainly had the makings of good relief workers in themselves were not accepted by Friends because of doubts about their ability to fit into a Quaker " discipline." And yet it was just some of these slightly angular people from a Quaker point of view who might have had the qualities of imaginative leadership that is so important in relief work. Friends would do well to ponder the later quotations from W. C. Braithwaite* and consider whether our Society is not more anxious to see that nobody is ever let into its life and work who is not just like those of us who are already in, than it is to accept the uncomfortable but creative help of those who might help us uncover new Truth.† We frequently lament our lack of the fire of the early Friends. May it not be that we fear the tension of a real ferment of provocative ideas coming from those whose experience of the love and power of God converges on, rather than runs along with, our own ?

* See p. 57 and p. 63.
† There were occasions when the attitude of Friends to non-Friends offering to do relief work seemed to be parallel to the attitude of my own meeting at the beginning of the nineteenth century. " J.H. reports that himself and E.W. accompanied by two women Friends have had an appointment with Elizabeth Box, and on consideration of her having had her education in the Society and conducting herself in a consistent manner are of the judgment that it may be safe to acknowledge her as a Member, with which this Meeting concurs." Hull Monthly Meeting, 21. v. 1807.

However that may be—and I commend it as an important line of thought—there was one quality which, when manifest, was quite incompatible with Friends relief work. That was hunger for personal power, or any sense of personal ambition. As one examines good Quaker service in the past, I believe it is this absence of any desire for power or prestige that is its most obvious and also, if I may say so, its most attractive feature. The healing quality of the Service has lain very largely in its lack of interest in anything other than the needs of victims. As a Society we have at our best sought no denominational power in relation to our Service. It is our very amateurishness that has, oddly enough, given us influence for nobody ever seems to be afraid of us. In so far as our predecessors won this confidence through true humility, let us be thankful for the tradition we have inherited and hope we may be worthy followers of it. But do not let us bask complacently in a reputation for inoffensiveness. By all means, let us not mix service with the hope of rewards. But parallel with our capacity to give relief work that seems to commend itself to our fellows because of its disinterestedness, I could wish that we were capable of preaching the word of the Lord in such a way that we might be in the tradition of the prophets. A true and complete sense of responsibility before God would not only subdue any temptation to strive after or maintain personal power ; it would also " drive us forth with the apostolic fervour of the early Church."

By this time it may look as if the selection of Quaker relief workers was a task for genii looking for saints. It was, of course, nothing of the sort. It was a blundering process in which many mistakes, positive and negative, were made. By the end, we were probably making fewer positive mistakes, but we may have been robbing ourselves of some of the wayward individualists of the kind who set things in motion in the early days when creation mattered more than system.

The sort of analysis of motives and behaviour that I have been making here was rarely in the forefront of the minds of working members of the Service. There were times when individuals or groups set out self-consciously to be good relief workers by thinking and doing all the proper things, and then there was almost always danger of an explosion from the intolerable tensions set up by such priggishness. If rising spirtual temperatures are not to lead to pointless explosions—as they sometimes did—they need either the most careful and sensitive treatment, or the draught of a great gust of laughter. The former sometimes came through a good Meeting for Worship, but this was more rare than the gust of laughter.

ADMINISTRATION

" Where freedom is not sought in independence, but in dependence on God, there the mastery over things will not lead to obsession by the things of the world or by technical powers ; there the freedom of the individual will not produce the dissolution of community ; there the structural hierarchy of competence based on unlikeness will not lead to an authoritarian caste-system or class-dominion ; there individual freedom and social cohesion will be balanced, because the recognition of equal dignity is combined with a functional aristocracy, the freedom of the individual and the interest of the individual being equally recognized." Emil Brunner. *Christianity and Civilization.* p. 141.

I come now to the third question which is begged when relief work is explained simply in terms of the Good Samaritan —the question of how hundreds of relief workers scattered over hundreds of miles and spending enormous sums of money can be effectively organized without putting their Samaritan instincts into intolerable straight-jackets. Christians have given far too little critical thought to this matter of administration and organization. They have tended to think either that good organization does not matter so long as the spirit is sound ; or they have taken over secular administrative ideas which have been as much moulded by material considerations, as by regard for the spiritual nature of the universe ; and while Friends have frequently fallen into one or other of these errors, yet within our heritage there is a tradition of really radical thinking about questions of administration and organization.

ADMINISTRATION IN QUAKER EXPERIENCE

George Fox and some of the wiser of the early Friends showed something like genius for devising methods of administration, which left the spirit truly free, yet preserved a sense of order within the group and between the Quaker group and its often hostile environment. Fox was one of the strongest advocates of proper record keeping. It was his

patient firmness which established a form of marriage cere-
mony so spiritually true that it survives with virtually no
alteration to this day, and so technically appropriate that,
though it did not conform to the strict legal requirements of
the time, it was yet pronounced valid by the courts as early as
1661. Fox was the creative mind behind the establishment
of a method of Church Government, much criticized by
many of his contemporaries, which is in good working order
to this day. Not only the distribution of business between our
various meetings for discipline, but the habit of making
minutes as the business proceeds and the habit of seeking for
the sense of the meeting and not taking votes, with all these
procedures worked out through worship, which does not
differ in essence from that of meetings specifically arranged
for worship—all this was seen from very nearly the beginning
of the Society. The Preface to the 1834 edition of Rules of
Discipline, of the Religious Society of Friends contains this
passage :

> " The history of these proceedings [the development of good
> administrative methods for the conduct of the affairs of the Society]
> affords no small evidence that the spirit of a sound mind influenced
> the body in its earliest periods ; contending as they did, for so
> large a measure of individual spiritual liberty and placing the
> authority of men, in religious matters, in a position so subordinate
> to that of the one Great Head of the church, they nevertheless
> recognized the importance and necessity of arrangements and of
> human instrumentality, under the direction of the Spirit of Christ,
> and they were led to establish a system of order at once so simple
> and efficient, that notwithstanding the varying circumstances of
> the Society, and the power of every annual meeting to alter it, it
> has been found in its main particular, adapted to those changes and
> it remains to this day essentially the same as it was within forty
> years of the rise of the Society."

One hundred and fifteen years later, there is no reason to
modify the last phrase of that extract.

To many Friends and others, John Woolman is the most
important Quaker figure of the eighteenth century. Like the
Good Samaritan, Francis of Assisi and others, he challenges us
to regard ourselves and our own interests, material security,

and aggrandisement as of no importance beside the divine call to give *ourselves* to ministering to the needs of the bodies and souls of others. In a way, John Woolman avoided the problem of administration. But he did not neglect it. He showed signs of being an excellent administrator, but, seeing that this would lead him to where he was not concerned to go, he deliberately refused to involve himself in the substantial economic and social enterprises which were open to him and chose to remain quite free as an individual, to lay before Friends his testimony about the wrongness of slavery and the dangers lurking in wealth. He rendered Christian service of a deep order, not merely to the Society of Friends or to the slaves, but to the whole human race through the inspired simplicity of his re-call to men to follow the spirit of Christ within. To have been the nursing mother of John Woolman was perhaps the greatest service of the eighteenth century Society of Friends.

But Christianity knows that God reaches out to men wherever they may be, and whatever they may be doing, and by faithful testimony and learning men may serve God in all sorts and conditions of society. There is no one pattern of human behaviour that is good. John Woolman ran the risk of shirking great outward responsibility ; by faithfulness his life was not retreat but noble discovery. Other Friends accepted the risks of successful organization ; their faithfulness is not less worthy of thankfulness.

Men and women throughout the world in the eighteenth century were desperately poor. Hunger, disease, dirt, squalor, suffering and degrading work made life hell for the many. Ghastly as were some of the results of the Industrial Revolution, and brutal as were some of the philosophical and religious attitudes associated with it, the growth of large-scale industry was a process which certainly held within it the possibility of liberating the bodies and souls of men from much physical and spiritual bondage. It is true that our inability to match material progress with growth in moral insight and self-control has led us into great difficulties. But that is not the fault of some of those Friends whose skill, organizing ability and profound social responsibility lay behind important aspects of the Industrial Revolution.

The development of the iron industry in the eighteenth century is to a great extent a story of Quaker brains and enterprise, and no family is more outstanding in this connection than the Darbys of Coalbrookdale. Industrial success is less unusual than the saintly devotion of a John Woolman, but the story of the great Quaker ironmasters, Abraham Darby II in particular, and of his son-in-law Richard Reynolds, is a story of technical discovery and of moral courage that can stand not unworthily alongside that of John Woolman. The world has abused the Darby heritage, as it has neglected the testimonies of Woolman. Both spoke nobly to their age as Christians who moved in close to the world's evils to fight them the more faithfully. Both speak searchingly to us.

Abraham Darby's father, originally a Bristol Friend, moved to Coalbrookdale in Shropshire where he discovered how to smelt iron with coal of which there was plenty, instead of charcoal, the supply of which was diminishing. He died when Abraham II was only six, and for the next thirty years, the Works were run by a relative who made further considerable technical advances and who does not appear to have had much " stop in his mind " about making canon. Abraham II began to share the management in 1732, and took control after 1745 ; the technical progress continued, and the Coalbrookdale works were among the most advanced and largest in the country ; but contracts for arms were deliberately refused in peace as well as during the Seven Years' War, and the American War of Independence. This policy continued under the direction of Richard Reynolds during the long French Wars of the Napoleonic era, and it was at this time that the Darbys and other Quaker firms were outdistanced by non-Quaker concerns which exploited the international situation. But Abraham Darby's sense of responsibility to the community was not limited to refusal to make arms. His great technical discovery was how to turn pig-iron into bar-iron, a discovery that opened up a whole new

phase of industrial development ; yet he felt it wrong to de-
prive the public of such an acquisition and took no
patents.

When Richard Reynolds took control, he insisted that the
furnaces should be stopped on Sundays in spite of all the
inconvenience and industrial disadvantage involved. And
when the price of iron rose during the American War, he
refused to raise the price in order to be clear of war-profiteering.
Indeed a small committee of customers was established to fix a
fair price. It was under Richard Reynolds that iron was
first used for the rails of wagon roads, and this was one of the
two parent discoveries which ultimately led to the invention
of railways. And about the turn of the century it was
cast-iron pipes from the Darby works that made possible
the extension of piped water supplies and the establishment
of gas distribution. Reynolds cared for his work-people
with equal imagination. He built good houses for the old
and the sick, as well as for the employed ; he established
schools, to get pupils for which he had to subsidize parents
who were suspicious of education ; he bought supplies
wholesale in times of famine, and sold them to his neighbours
at a fair price. And when he retired, inevitably a rich man,
Richard Reynolds set about distributing his money, since he
disapproved of the idea of making bequests by will. He gave
enormous sums away, but often anonymously and often
through others whose judgment he trusted but who had not
money of their own to give where they knew it was needed.
There is no doubt at all about the social sense, the integrity,
the technical and organizing ability, and the Christian
neighbourliness of these eighteenth century Quaker indus-
trialists.

Abraham Darby II, Woolman and Reynolds—who incidentally was clerk of Yearly Meeting in 1786—were all born
within twenty-five years of one another. They lived through
the restless decades of hitherto unparalleled world-restlessness
and industrial creation. They were essentially of their age,
and yet they were in no way swamped by it. And I believe
that they represent two aspects of our heritage that have been

drawn together in Quaker relief work. To the extent that those who have done the work have given up their prospects, security and comfort for conscience sake and have been drawn into the ministry of personal service they have followed, however haltingly and fearfully, in the steps of Woolman. And in a measure they had the freedom of Woolman, loosed from the bonds of " cumber " and therefore free to come and go according to the Lord's will—a freedom needing some maturity of the spirit truly to enjoy. To the extent that the work has involved very complex administration with much ingenuity and invention in the use of large corporate resources in unprecedented circumstances, there has been something of the spirit of the Quaker pioneers who served in the Industrial Revolution. Nobody would claim that the individual characters of the relief workers were particularly outstanding.*
It was, I believe, through the combination with a measure of vitality of the two traditions that we were able corporately to do a modest job, amateur and untidy in many respects, but much beyond what might have been expected if the participating individuals had been assessed separately.

THE ADMINISTRATIVE PROBLEM OF FRIENDS RELIEF SERVICE.

As an executive organization spread over a very wide area, the Friends Relief Service of the Second World War had to be able to act with the precision and certainty of a well-run business if it was not to waste the money of subcribers. As a group of amateurs each with a personal concern for relief work, serving under the Society of Friends, which itself had a corporate concern for relief work, there was liable to be much confusion about who was responsible for what and to whom. In the course of its existence the Relief Service hammered out a form of organization which was an attempt to relate this basis of concern to the needs of executive efficiency in an undertaking of some size.

* " Second-rate work by third-rate people " was somebody's description of Quaker work in the first world war. *Vide* A. Ruth Fry, *A Quaker Adventure :* Introduction.

First of all, let us have a look at what the Service actually was. It was responsible for the diverse social service work of members whose numbers varied at any one time from under 200 to over 500 scattered about all over this country from 1940 to 1946, and over a good deal of Europe from 1944 to 1948. Most of the members were youngish men and women ; some had held posts of considerable responsibility in civilian life ; others came from quite humble occupations ; a few had professional qualifications ; some came straight from their studies. The majority had no previous experience or training which fitted them for work in the Service ; in this respect the Service was very like the war-time army. Like the army, it had to build itself up quickly from a mass of assorted " bodies " ; unlike the army, it started with no experience at all. It began in November, 1940, with the appointment of a secretary and a part-time clerical assistant.

Responsibility within the organization bore no direct relationship to pay. There was no financial inducement. Certain basic amounts were available to all—board and lodging plus a standard pocket-money and civilian clothing allowance which rose with rising prices from 10s. a week in 1941 to 17s. 6d. in 1947. Members with family responsibilities received additional financial support if necessary. But nobody ever received commercial rates, nobody ever received more pay because of good work (or less pay because of bad work) and there was no system of promotion. Neither was there any security. Everybody was accepted only on the understanding that if there was no useful work for which he or she was suitable then he or she would be asked to leave the Service.

The ultimately responsible body was the whole body of Quakers in Great Britain, meeting annually at the Yearly Meeting. The immediately responsible body was a Main Committee, appointed by and responsible to Meeting for Sufferings, the representative gathering of the Society of Friends in Great Britain meeting monthly, and dealing with every aspect of Quaker life and thought. The Main Committee was composed of 30-40 Friends, varying in age from

about 21 to 70-plus ; very few of whom at first, but a substantial minority of whom later, had first-hand experience of
the relief work. The Committee met monthly for about
2½ hours. There was a sub-committee of this Main Committee, with various titles and responsibilities, but mostly
composed of working members of the Service, with considerable day-to-day knowledge, which met weekly or fortnightly
for administrative business.

The Service was a body which differed considerably from
any other form of executive organization, whether govern-
mental, public or private enterprise, school, hospital, or
voluntary social service. For instance, every Quaker in the
Service was by virtue of membership of the Society of Friends,
a member of the ultimate governing body, Yearly Meeting,
not by representation but in person, able to take part vocally
in its proceedings. Therefore, in principle, any Quaker
member of the Service was in a constitutional position to
challenge the authority of any senior on whom he depended
for his orders.

The basis of the work in personal " concern " has already
been referred to ; so has the selection of personnel, a process
in which we had to be convinced by the volunteer's attitude
to and understanding of relief work done by a Christian
society, while we had also to assess their likely ability in some
practical job to which hitherto they had probably been
strangers. And while both assessments were important,
there was more room for adjustment when we made errors in
the latter than when we made them in the former.

Now, when a plumber, an accountant, a nurse, a personnel
manager, a cook, a telephone operator or the warden of an
evacuation hostel are appointed by a private or public
employer, they are appointed for specific duties, and provided
they fulfil those duties, their responsibility is ended. If they
are good at getting on with other people, so much the better ;
if they quarrel with other people, they may have to go, however good they are at their technical job. But it is not
ordinarily the business of any one of them as an employee to
have views on how they shall all be co-ordinated, or on how

34

the tasks shall be selected which, as an organization, they are to undertake. It is the job of the management to take responsibility for the general direction of the concern. A wise management will consult and inform subordinates and will attempt to draw them into policy making : it is no part of orthodox administrative theory that every member of the concern has equal moral responsibility for policy. But this is precisely where the F.R.S. was so different. Undertaking work " under concern " means that the whole service is the Lord's and puts the Chairman, the General Secretary, the shorthand typist, the lorry-driver, the storekeeper, the doctor and the accountant under an equal moral and spiritual commitment. And because as we recognize in the whole of our Quaker method of meeting for worship and for discipline, there is equality before the Lord, so there was an equality of responsibility in F.R.S. which invalidated all orthodox conceptions of executive relationships. For in the work of the Lord the most junior member of the Service had a moral obligation to take responsibility for ends, and therefore for means, and unless he did take this responsibility, the service ceased to express that part of its nature which was rooted in personal service under concern.

Yet plainly this moral responsibility with its element of active participation in the determination of policy is not easily compatible with administrative order and economy of effort, which involve defined responsibility in specified spheres and a readiness to obey instructions on the part of those with subordinate functions.

Before looking further at the actual administrative pattern, it will be well to look at the various elements that had to be woven into the pattern.

YEARLY MEETING

First of all there is the Society of Friends itself, 20,000 strong, grouped into four hundred meetings in Great Britain. Its governing body, Yearly Meeting, can be attended by the whole 20,000. In fact, about 750 usually choose to come. Any Friend, young or old, may take part in its deliberations vocally, as well as by outwardly silent presence. Its sessions, as are all business meetings of the Society, are basically periods of worship, in which resolutions, set speeches, and aggressive advocacy of particular policy, are out of place. It meets for the Worship of God, and while any given session is devoted to some aspect of thought or service, the contributions should build up towards a sense of the meeting as it waits for the guidance of God in the particular field under consideration. Yearly Meeting is not, in the last resort, made up of a body of experts. People who know a great deal about the matter in hand may do most of the talking, central committee members familiar with the complexities of translating convictions into practical terms, may appear to be leading the meeting. But a few halting yet sincere hesitations, uttered by a Friend from a small meeting in a distant county may, in fact, be of more significance in revealing a matter in its true setting than all the sophistication of the committee worthies. Again and again on deep issues it is reality as known and experienced by the simple and single-minded meeting, that does not know too much to have lost its simple faith, that guides the Society ; and the central Committee or its administrator who knows that its service is, in the end, related to the life of the local meetings in the country, will have a deep respect for the weight of Yearly Meeting.

But plainly, Yearly Meeting cannot decide everything. It only meets once a year ; it can only handle matters which are presented to it in such a way that it can understand or think it understands them. Therefore what is to be presented to it needs the most careful selection. It should not be trivial, or the meeting will fail to give any substantial response ; it should not be " window-dressing " or the meeting will either reject it for what it is, or, temporarily misled, will give it a hollow approval ; it should not be so ill-digested by those responsible for presentation that Yearly Meeting has neither time nor ability to sort the issues out ; it can only handle what is suitable for handling by such a large and, in a sense, casual body. And yet its handling must be real, for the corporate work and testimony of the Society is, by its very nature, the result of corporate guidance reached in Worship.

If a Committee hides from Yearly Meeting the truth of its work, its work will be bad. It is not difficult, in the short run, to confuse or hoodwink Yearly Meeting. But to just the degree that this is done, those responsible are not laying their service before the Lord in Worship, and the work will not be what it purports to be. It becomes something else—the expression of the unanchored intelligences of the members, of the ambition of individuals, of the unreflective traditionalism of those who have ceased to think critically of what they are doing. Yearly Meeting wants to come to a sense of the meeting about what is being done in its name. A good and sensitive committee will present its material helpfully because it has itself been aware of the need to develop its sense of the meeting under the guidance of God. It is one of the more remarkable evidences of the unifying and creative powers of God, that a large gathering like Yearly Meeting can often almost effortlessly pick up a thread from any small group of its members who have truly wrestled and prayed beforehand about matters that were ripe for presentation to the large body. As a simple matter of experience, Yearly Meeting in a waiting and worshipping state is a wonderfully sure judge of what is truly of the Lord and what is merely notional, however intelligent.

To mortal man and fallible committees, all of whom often want to outrun the measure of their gifts, Yearly Meeting can be a sore trial. It can be very slow, even at times of true inspiration ; it can be incalculable, either because material is badly presented, or because it is tired, or because its own membership is not faithful. Its greatest potential danger, however, is that which springs from the conservatism of successful institutions. The Society of Friends has become a very respectable body with a reputation, just or unjust, for sound judgment and honest dealing in important matters. It is this reputation, built up over generations, by the work and character of our spiritual ancestors, that gives the current generation immense initial advantages in anything they undertake. To represent a Quaker organization is quite an adequate introduction to any civilian or war ministry over half the globe. This is a reputation not lightly to be thrown away, and understandably enough, there is a tendency for Yearly Meeting and all the official organs of the Society to regard themselves as the guardians of a proved tradition. A good tradition is built up on long experience of finding the right answers ; which is natural enough, for Truth is eternal and its discovered aspects are transmitted down the generations by traditions and institutions. But where this has been done with a measure of purity there comes in a paradoxical element of inertia, often disguised as stability, which expresses itself as a strong though quite unconscious desire to " stay put." The Society often likes to think of itself as revolutionary. But, as Bagehot said of the British people, " It only comprehends what is familiar to it—what comes into its own experience, what squares with its own thoughts."*

At Yearly Meeting in 1948 Friends were shocked by an outspoken assertion from a former member of the Relief Service that there was a great gulf between young and old in the Society and that the latter were failing to share their experience with the former ; that they did not, indeed, realize that the former were fainting for thirst. The Friend added that all members of the Relief Service would know what he meant when he said that there was something radically wrong. I believe that I know what he was talking about, though I think it was a red herring to drag in the difference of generations. What I believe he meant to emphasize was this element of conservatism that makes it difficult for a respectable institution like our Society to realize that it may find its own internal structure so cosy that it forgets that it lives in a rapidly changing world,—partly because it does not *want* to remember this. This is the priestly and levitical side of our corporate life. And as some of us staggered up and down a messy world in the Relief Service we often felt that the Society had not the faintest idea how to lead us because it had turned in on itself, and had sought security in its institutional self-righteousness.

* Bagehot, *English Constitution*, Ch. V.

The distinction between the expression of eternal Truth and the expression of sociological conservatism is extraordinarily difficult to detect at any given moment.   But it is a distinction of which the Society is barely aware, and it is because conservatism is usually hailed as attachment to Truth that relief workers and others pre-occupied with change, have often felt themselves at odds with Yearly Meeting and the Society as a whole. Perhaps the situation may be summed up by recalling Neave Brayshaw's use of the rhyme about the little girl who had a little curl, for describing a Friends' meeting, which may be very very good or may be horrid. The corporate sense of the Society can move mountains when truly inspired. It is exasperating beyond measure when mouthing Quaker platitudes as a defence against radical thinking about changing situations. Here is the strength and weakness of the Society and its Yearly Meeting as a body responsible for social action. And no human institution is a good judge of its own moods and motives, the less so when all men speak well of it.

THE COMMITTEE

The second element in the web of responsibility was the Committee, a group of 30-40 Friends, meeting monthly, with the continuous duty of formulating policy and supervising its execution. It was the body which had formally to crystallize the sense of the Society, when the Society was not in session, to know what should be simply reported to Meeting for Sufferings, or Yearly Meeting, and what should be referred to one of the larger bodies for decision. In this respect it was concerned with simplifying issues to their outlines. On the other hand, it had to know enough of the perplexities and possible alternative courses of action, and of the weaknesses and failures in execution to be able to take responsibility for guiding and controlling what was actually done. It had a singularly difficult job, for the Society expected it to know everything, while the members of the Service knew that the Committee actually knew very little and could not possibly know much. Time was always against it. An important committee must come to grips with some detail, and yet the length and frequency of its meetings were limited by the heavy claims on the time of its experienced Quaker members.

At one period, the load was lightened by the establishment of a weekly executive committee, composed largely of working members of the Service. As a committee it had great technical value by virtue of its composition, since it included most of the heads of executive departments, who knew each other's business, strengths and weaknesses, sufficiently well to be effective critics of one another, and who could talk in the shorthand of men and women on the job, and so cover much ground quickly. In my own view this committee which lasted for about a year in 1942-43 was a most effective executive body for the administration of relief work. Its greatest weakness was that, with an average age of about thirty, it lacked maturity of judgment and the weight in the things of the spirit that an older group of Friends would have had. It probably came to decisions too easily in the light of " good business " and not sufficiently in the light of the Lord. Rightly or wrongly it simply did not carry the confidence of Committee and Yearly Meeting Friends. Given time and responsibility and imaginative encouragement, I believe its members would have grown in corporate and individual stature; but it was cut off in its youth. It is perhaps a prejudiced view to say that this was because it was incompatible with the traditional pattern of Quaker administration.

And so the overburdening of the Main Committee began again, though the actual conduct of its business was eased by its insistence on an efficient system, in scale probably unparalleled in the history of the Society, of circulating papers in advance. On its own level, this system worked really well ; it would not have done so without first-rate administrative ability in the office, keeping the flow of business steadily moving through appropriate sub-committees, producing minutes, memoranda and agenda. Committee administration is not an exciting occupation, and Friends should realize what they owe to those who are prepared to live among files and minutes, while their fellow-workers struggle with excitements, successes, and failures on the field, while some of their fellow-administrators have the pleasure of visiting existing, and planning new work, and while the Society as a whole basks in the glory of a job which wins wide commendation.

But while a system of committees and sub-committees held together very largely by good paper work, can provide co-ordination, it does not provide inspiration. By the time our committee had dealt with what *had* to be decided there was little time for either worship or thought.

ADMINISTRATORS

The third element was the group of administrators, mostly working from Friends House.

It was the contribution of the administrators that could most quickly vitiate the quality of the Service; for if the administrators lacked effective sensitiveness, on the one hand to the concern of the Society, and on the other to the concern and needs of the members in the field, then the very basis of the Service was destroyed. For it rested on the generalized concern of the Society to relieve suffering being coincident with the particular concern of individuals also to relieve suffering. The reduction of these converging concerns to some sort of practicable shape was a matter of administration. It was the administrators who personified the " concern of the Society " to the man on the job who might never see a Quaker meeting where he was working. And it was on the awareness of the administrator of what sort of backing the man on the job wanted, and on the administrator's ability to convey this awareness to the Society, that there depended the capacity of the Society to make its vague sense of concern specifically relevant to what field workers were trying to do. To put the matter concretely; the Society would never have become interested in old people if its general concern for service had not led to a number of young members becoming deeply involved in the care of aged evacuees. For three years there were few signs that the Society cared in any specific way, but then, quite suddenly, the experience of the field workers took hold of Friends generally, and it became clear that here was something vital. Throughout that three years, it was mostly the administrators who had to carry the responsibility of transforming the unformulated concern of the Society into administrative shape suitable for supporting members' individual concern, also unformulated originally, but which had now become specific. In an overseas field, the development of the work was almost always perceived more sharply by those working on the spot ; but it could also be easily perceived lop-sidedly. An enormous amount depended on the ability of the administrators to pick up the stirrings on the field and align them with possible stirrings in the Society at home ; and equally on their ability to extract from the Society at home a formulated or unformulated sense of backing to those in the field and convey it to them, quite possibly combined with basically uncongenial policy decisions.

It was the business of administrators to know a great deal in general, to give people working in the field the support and supplies that were needed when they were needed, to relate one piece of work to another, and to see what situations were likely to call for attention at varying dates in the future and to propose plans accordingly. They always knew more about the work than committee members ; they were usually in a position to see further in the first instance. They had, therefore, a responsibility for giving committees a lead, and it would have been unnatural if they had not usually wanted to move at a rather different pace from that at which the committees were prepared to go.

On the other hand, the administrators were more concerned with tidiness and good order than were people in the field, who were faced with actual distress which could often only be met by resourceful unorthodoxy and adaptability. The essence of administration is to reduce the amount of laborious thinking necessary to carry anything on by making as much as possible subject to standard treatment. This saves wear, tear and time, and a good administrator can produce an organization in which everybody knows exactly what is required of him in relation to what everybody else is doing. But in relief work the people in the field are continually meeting the unprecedented ; and they often feel, quite truly, that their responsibility for answering a need must take precedence over general administrative tidiness blessed by Friends House. A loyal mercenary who is paid to apply the rules is very reliable in one sense. But a relief worker's loyalty is to the inspiration of God, and there is a real difficulty in believing that this is heard more distinctly or more frequently in Friends House than elsewhere. For the bureaucrat, the highest achievement is the smooth running of the machine he has created for a purpose. Unprecedented needs, leading to new or changing purposes, may throw his mechanism out of gear, and the bureaucrat at the seat of policy-making will tend to select or perpetuate purposes that suit the smooth running of his machine. This is the continual temptation of the administrator, and we often stumbled—though, equally, the man on the spot often overestimated the local variation and would have done well to keep the rules.

Above all, the administrator was subject to the temptation of power.

FIELD AND OFFICE WORKERS

The fourth element was the group of field workers and rank and file in the office who had no direct part in the making of committee policy, but through whose work the concern of the Society was actually expressed among those in need. Some of these were the members who day by day offered cups of cold water in the name of Christ to the needy, and if theirs was the service which, when things went well, gave the richest sense of reward, it was also sometimes a very lonely service and the service whose failure could be most bitter, especially if failure was felt to be due to weakness, obstinacy, or lack of imagination elsewhere. And there were those, like the packers of clothes and shorthand typists, and motor mechanics, who neither saw the work whole, nor handed the cup. It was hard for them to be sure that their sense of

43

concern was adequately incorporated into the Service. All of these members could easily magnify their opportunities, achievements and frustrations beyond what was reasonable in the light of the Service as a whole ; and yet without their vital sense of concern all the Yearly Meeting, Committee and Friends House policy-making would have been barren.

CORPORATE RESPONSIBILITY

So here were the four elements with responsibility for the job ; at one end the Society—at its best, sensitive and creative, but burdened with a respectable conservatism in consequence of its organizational success, and with, as a former Clerk of Yearly Meeting once observed, a very high ratio of hot-water bottles per foot; at the other, some hundreds of young men and women under personal concern, attempting to answer to " that of God in every man " in the places where they found themselves, which were often places of want, fear, insecurity and degradation, but were also sometimes rich in the experience of God's outreaching love. The gulf between Friends at home and the field was often as wide as that between club armchairs and desert fighting. In between, were Committees and administrators, with some capacity for seeing both sides, yet pressed by time and function to act expediently rather than rightly. Somehow these elements had to be brought together in a pattern providing at the same time for the free blowing of the spirit and for the complicated organizational order necessary to get anything done in a world at once both chaotically disorganized and tightly controlled. No assertion of the supremacy of any outward authority would meet the need, for each individual's status was rooted in his own sense of " concern " and not in his position within the organization as the superior of so-and-so, and the junior to what's-his-name. To do something or to refrain *because* Yearly Meeting says so, with a shrug of the shoulders as a gesture of repudiation of moral responsibility, is quite contrary to the principles on which the Society of Friends tries to preserve administrative order.

To perceive the lines on which the unity between personal concern and administrative order can be reached, a distinction must be made between moral and administrative responsibility. To determine what shall be done and the quality of spirit in which ends shall be pursued, is a moral responsibility ; to determine how that shall be done and to see that it is done, is an administrative responsibility within the moral framework. Moral responsibility is found by Friends through " the sense of the Meeting." Administrative responsibility in complex matters is taken by individuals given the task of translating the " sense of the Meeting " into action, being guided all along by the moral obligation to remain true to the " sense of the Meeting."

In the relief service, moral responsibility was equal between all members of the Society, and all members of the Service. Ends and intentions were matters for decision in a spirit of worship. Administrative action followed, taken by groups and individuals given appropriate and defined status for exercising authority. But it took us a long time to see that the basis of relationships in this sort of work could never be that of employer to employee. For it was not easy to bring ourselves out of the traditional secular atmosphere of executive organization where superiors tell juniors to go and come, where superiors take all moral responsibility and expect juniors and employees to do as they are told. For after all, the Committee *was* formally responsible for all action, without qualification, and in these circumstances it seemed obvious that those serving under it must accept its rulings.

REPRESENTATIVE CONFERENCE

But as the work developed it became plainer and plainer that the concern of individual workers and the corporate concern of groups of workers was at least as fundamental to right service as the formal authority of the Committee, and no system of organization which did not recognize this could possibly have real vitality. So in 1942 a " representative conference " was called over a week-end at Birmingham.

45

The membership consisted of about 24 members actually engaged in field work, chosen by their fellow-workers in the field, of about 8 members engaged in day-to-day administration at the centre, of about 8 Friends who were members of the Committee, or other Friends of standing in the Society.

The purpose of the Conference was corporately to look at major and minor issues of the service, which any concerned felt should be raised. Those coming from the field had had an opportunity of preparing and presenting minutes drawn up by those who appointed them, and the agenda was itself, therefore, a corporate affair. The conference was felt to have been a success to the extent that it did actually deal with real issues in such a way as was felt to be *right*. I think nobody went away feeling beaten ; though we had come together with different backgrounds of service and Quaker experience, yet we separated with a sense of having seen the same things in the same way. There was, in fact, an objectivity about the proceedings which was exactly what had been hoped for, an objectivity that represented our recognition of the existence of a Will of God that was real for the whole group and that implied derivative obligations on each one of us.

Having achieved this sense of unity, not in vague terms, but in relation to actual issues facing the Service it was possible for the executive officers, for the functional sub-committees, and for the main committee itself to exercise their administrative authority without domination. Moral and administrative responsibility were seen to be separate things, but the latter was derived from the former which, securely rooted in a sense of worship, was free, yet neither capricious nor anarchic.

Subsequently a similar type of conference was held about every six months at home, and in a modified form, the same procedure was followed in several of the overseas fields, later on.

There were a number of important points to note about these gatherings. They never had any executive authority ; their status was purely advisory. The constitutional responsibility of the Main Committee, of Meeting for Sufferings, or of Yearly Meeting, was never impaired except, possibly, in one respect. The Conference asked for and obtained the right regularly to review, and if thought well, to revise the appointment of the senior executive officer of the Service. This was entirely appropriate since it is at the senior administrative level that the hierarchical administrative system begins to take shape in relation to the equality of moral responsibility among all Friends and all members of the Service. But no complication was introduced into the straight descent of executive responsibility within the administration.

The Representative Conferences, for all their lack of status were much the most important gatherings in the life of the Service—far more important than the Main Committee. I doubt very much whether many members of the Committee or of Yearly Meeting realized how important they were ; and certainly their significance was never formalized. It was as great as it was simply because the Representative Conference was an institution which never claimed power ; it was quite ready to allow informed conviction, worked out under the guidance of God, to find its own ways of carrying weight.

In essence, what happened was that by one channel or another, no matter of current or prospective principle or practice that was causing substantial thought within the Service, failed to be brought to the Agenda. It might be a question of the shape work should take abroad and relationships with armies ; it might be the matter of what was the right system of financial allowances ; it might be the way in which members should be kept informed of Service developments ; it might be the place of corporate worship in a working group ; it might be the question of by what descriptive title certain members should be known—was " Stores-officer " more or less military than " Quartermaster " ?

The Conference met over a whole week-end and it was prepared to work hard and fast, but avoided hurry. To manage this involved careful organization. For organization, provided it is neither top-heavy nor an end in itself, is the greatest liberator of the spirit. Both John Woolman and Richard Reynolds took great trouble to organize their affairs so that their spirits were free. In our Representative

47

Conferences a great deal of effort went on beforehand in sorting matters into an effective agenda, and the clerks came to have a timetable which allocated time to the various subjects in accordance with their estimated weight, perhaps five or six items in a two-hour session. The timetable was not inflexible ; if substantial matter would not be fitted in, then more time was given ; but all knew the general plan, and, with an absence of group or individual " tactics," shape was retained. A vast deal of paper work was done in advance by the circulation of reports and of minutes from working sections ; and everybody present was not only assumed to have read and digested this material, but had in fact done so. The Conference sat at tables, so that the papers could be handled. The marshalling of the material and the formation of the agenda were done by members appointed by the previous conference ; they did not represent any particular approach to the work of the Service. The Clerk came also to be appointed by a nominating committee of the preceding conference. He or she might be an officer of the Committee, a member of the Service itself or an outside Friend. The Clerk was not in any sense a representative of any particular strand of policy in the Service. He was some Friend of character who held the confidence both of those with strong individualistic tendencies and of those whose outlook was tinged with age or caution. The Conference was therefore a body designed to deal with issues " timely and impartially " and from the first was felt, in fact, to be such.

Opening and subsequent exposition was usually short, and because of the very extensive practical knowledge of the issues, discussion was highly relevant. Criticism was more trenchant than in most Quaker gatherings, partly because the Service membership was, in a remarkable degree " knit unto the Lord, and unto one another," so that plain speaking was no embarrassment. The clerk made the minutes as the meeting proceeded, as at Yearly Meeting ; but since most of the issues were concrete and involved decisions regarding action that was expected to follow, the minutes were usually precise and the wording was carefully considered.

The advisory decisions of the Conference recorded in minutes were passed to the appropriate executive agencies, the main committee, sub-committee, or administrative officers. It would be too much to say that they were always acted on, but this was for reasons of lethargy, lack of time, or unavailability of personnel rather than because they were not acceptable to the executive agencies concerned. It was indeed at these conferences that the true thinking of the Service was done, and subsequent committee decisions were reflections of attitudes already reached at the conferences.

But none of these devices and none of these procedures would have been effective in preserving order among 500 people scattered over hundreds of miles, and doing scores of jobs, all of them volunteers, a good many of them with a strong streak of anarchy in relation to administration, and no system of discipline based on any sort of sanction, except the very rare request to leave the Service—such a group was not and could not have been held together on any mere committee system. The structure, with all its elaborate machinery, stood, I believe, because at its heart there was a conviction that " there is a Will of God in every situation " and that the Will of God can be found as a quite objective determinant by those who, sometimes alone and sometimes in company, wait and search for it, with the spirit of Jesus Christ as their guide.

In fact, we quickly found that the conference reached a quality of peace and unity not given by the world, in which our conception of service was broadened and deepened so that all holy desires, all good counsels, and all just works were known to be of God ; and self-consciousness of our individual separateness fell away. We talked plenty of rubbish, of course, but I cannot remember that we ever broke up without knowing that our foolishness and limitations had been transcended, if not completely, yet sufficiently to give us a glimpse of the reality of the purpose of God, and of our dependence on it. There was a freedom and a quality of participation that could not have existed had we remained conscious of our differences of age, function and experience.

It was not that we all came to those gatherings in an ideal frame of mind. Some of us were irritable and had matters of complaint in the forefront of our minds ; and others of us had been fiercely busy with matters of administration or personal relationships ; others of us had come with plans of our own, or of a group, that we felt should figure prominently. We had all the weaknesses of human kind. But we had also a glimmering of God's leading and we found the truth of Robert Barclay's account of Meeting for Worship, even though there was little outward silence in our business sessions.

> " Such is the evident Certainty of that Divine Strength, that is communicated by thus Meeting together, and Waiting in silence upon God ; that sometimes, when one hath come in, that hath been Unwatchful, and Wandering in his Mind, or suddenly out of the Hurry of outward Business, and so not inwardly gathered with the rest, so soon as he retires himself inwardly, this Power being in a good measure raised in the whole Meeting, will suddenly lay hold upon his Spirit, and wonderfully help to raise up the good in him, and beget him into the sense of the same Power, to the melting and warming of his heart ; even as the Warmth would take hold upon a man that is cold, coming into a Stove ; or as a Flame will lay hold upon some little Combustible Matter being near unto it. . . .
>
> Our Work then and Worship is, when we Meet together, for every one to Watch, and Wait upon God in themselves, and to be gathered from all Visibles thereinto. And as everyone is thus stated, they come to find the Good arise over the Evil, and the Pure over the Impure, in which God reveals himself, and draweth near to every Individual, and so be in the midst of the general ; Whereby each not only partakes of the particular Refreshment and Strength, which comes from the good in himself ; but is a sharer of the whole Body, as being a living Member of the Body, having a joint Fellowship and Communion with all."*

It was primarily in our Representative Conferences that we came to have this sense of being sharers of the whole Body, having a joint Fellowship and Communion with all. It was in so far as the whole Society is a working, waiting, and worshipping fellowship that it could gather up its own short-comings and those of its relief workers and set the whole under the guidance of God. At any given moment there will be individual and group unfaithfulness and weakness ; we did

* Apology, Proposition XI.

and do fail locally to work, wait and worship ; but so long as there is a Christian fellowship to which we belong, there is a stove to which we may come for that divine heating and inspiring warmth of which Barclay speaks. So long as the Society of Friends worships anywhere, those within its fellowship are not cut off from God's flame and warmth.

Even while the Representative Conference was an occasion for resolving the confusions and tensions which we brought to it, and even while, by hard though refreshing exercise of the spirit, we left the Conference better men and women than when we came, it would be a mistake to suppose that we always lived at this height when trying to translate our moral responsibility into administrative terms. There were tremendous strains within the Service and between the Service and its Committees, and the Society itself, arising partly from the rub of personality on personality, partly from the different proportions in which different groups saw the same issue, partly because of bad adjustment, incompetent administration and sheer thoughtlessness. Part of the strain arose from the practical difficulty of knowing when an issue was a moral one, to be determined by the sense of Divine Guidance and when it was an administrative one, to be determined by the appropriate executive officer or functional committee in the light of technical, financial or organizational good sense. More of this special problem is said later. In relation to strain on senior administrators, there is a vast deal to be said for the ordinary economic and professional systems, where there is no common moral responsibility, and where administrative responsibility is clearly determined at each level by the relatively easily defined and objective considerations of pay and status. Running an organization on Love and the Will of God is wearing work on all concerned. There is a true peace to be found in it, but it is indeed a peace which the world does not give.

EQUALITY AND HIERARCHY

So much for the general method whereby those actually doing the work and those in whose organizational name it was done, were, in a measure, brought together to determine moral and general administrative issues. But the subject cannot be left here, for the principles and practices disclosed by this analysis directly affected personal relationships between members of the Service. If there was moral equality between member and member, how could there, simultaneously, be a relationship of administrative seniority and subordination, the relationship being further complicated by the absence of differential pay or seniority arising from age or length of service ? What constitutes proper leadership in such an organization ? How is discipline maintained ? These questions must be considered.

PERSONAL RELATIONSHIPS

Plainly there could be no ranks. And yet there had to be a chain of administrative authority, so that, at any given moment, it was clear who was responsible for what. There must therefore be the usual sequence of wider and lesser responsibilities, with no casual querying by juniors of the decisions of seniors. But if, at any point, the administrative action of a senior appeared to be going beyond the limits of " the sense of the meeting " then an appropriate occasion must be taken by the whole group for looking at the situation. Therefore administrative action was always subject to the over-riding claims and necessities of the moral responsibility of the whole group. And yet if the claims of the latter were excessively asserted there would plainly be administrative stalemate. This, of course, involved an element of real or potential tension that was puzzling to those who did not understand what was happening. For instance, where the situation was healthy, fellow-members could talk not only to, but of one another, with great detachment. It was possible for fellow-members to analyse weak elements in one another's abilities without any sense of disloyalty or embarrassment. The casual or conventional observer might regard this as intrigue—as it could, of course, all too easily become, and sometimes did. But it was not usually, much less necessarily, so. In essence, it is a thoroughly healthy process, necessary, provided that it is truly enough done, to relate equal moral responsibility to unequal administrative responsibility. For where the two come into conflict, the cause of the trouble may be administrative weakness, and in that event the only thing to do is to look at the situation quite objectively to see what possible administrative plumbing, carpentry, or redesigning can be done. Given this capacity for objective consideration of personal response to the needs of the situation and the courage to act on the findings, stalemate is rare.

But there is one central condition of success in handling this potential tension between the same people in different mutual relationships—the freedom of each member from any lust for power, already mentioned several times. This seems to me almost, if not quite, the only weakness that disqualifies absolutely for Quaker Service as it should be—and for the very simple reason that those with ambition for power cannot see the work as the Lord's and themselves as His servants for Him to use as He wills. They cannot consider objectively the situation and what is demanded by it of all those involved in it. For them, prestige, authority, status, successful personal manipulation, matter more than God's will. And that will not do in a company of God's servants.

But this does *not* mean that there can be any shrinking from administrative responsibility. That must be taken with fearlessness, since the one sure way of failing to fulfil a purpose is to retreat from responsibility. Where there is a task to be done somebody must carry administrative responsibility for it, and precisely because moral responsibility was common to all members, there was in F.R.S. an insistence beyond the normal on the assumption of administrative responsibility, since the first people to note abdication from it were the rank and file and those frustrated for lack of it.

How then is readiness to take responsibility distinguished from ambition and lust for power? A technical answer might be found in the jargon of psychology, but in the Relief Service, the answer was easy to find, though often difficult to handle. The group could tell in a very short time who was interested in power for its own sake, and who was prepared to take responsibility if it made sense to take it, but who was quite detached about it. But while it was not difficult in practice to tell who was " in the life " and who was not, it was not nearly so easy to tell in advance.

The answer then, to this question of mutual relationships is that there is always an element of tension between those who are morally equal but carry unequal administrative responsibility, and that there is no sense in pretending that this tension does not exist. We are much too anxious to abolish tensions, whose right preservation is the very essence of true living. This particular tension is exhilarating just in so far as individuals are prepared to view their mutual relationships as those of fallible mortals who yet recognize that God has a purpose for them in the light of which their respective duties can be sorted out.

LEADERSHIP

This brings us to a consideration of the nature of leadership in the Society of Friends.

Leadership is a singularly ambiguous word, denoting all kinds of different relationships between groups and those who command, direct, inspire, stimulate, or integrate group activity, or combine some or all of these functions. At one end of the scale, a leader is the despotic head of a Nazi state ; at the other the leader of an orchestra has a purely æsthetic function and even that is subordinate to the direction of the conductor. One officer may be called by a title indicating leadership, while it is generally recognized that the " real " leadership resides elsewhere. Moreover, a well-led group may have many leaders, and may be able to reshuffle their functions with no organic break, indicating considerable skill in the handling of relationships between leaders. A healthy group should be able to change leaders when the group function changes, without disrupting the life of the group. A function of good leadership is to facilitate appropriate change.

The complexity of leadership was demonstrated when, say, a relief team appointed to do an emergency job, expected to be of short duration, found themselves still there six months later, with a long-term social problem on their hands and no obvious way out. If the team tackled the long-term job successfully, it was because the leadership abilities displayed in a " blitz " situation had given way to the different leadership abilities needed to hold a group together in a situation where development must be slow. The same individuals might or might not be prominent, but if these subsequently required abilities had not been there or could not have found a way of expressing themselves because of the rigidity of the group's administrative structure, then the group would have fallen apart as a working organism. In a lively group, aware of its purpose in terms of work to be done rather than in terms of its own formal shape, there will always be a tendency for the expression of leadership to take forms peculiarly suited to the matter in hand. Flexibility in drawing on sources of initiative and in integrating new ideas into appropriate patterns is essential ; but so is a reasonable measure of constancy in external relationships. Frequent changes in the person or committee representing the group to the outside world are disastrous. Yet to preserve outward stability while undergoing substantial internal adjustments leading to changing policies puts a considerable strain on the group's public representative who must express changing attitudes without appearing to be a weathercock. In a dynamic society, tension is inescapable between the need for a steady vehicle of expression of the group contribution, and the constant internal readjustment necessary to meet developing purposes.

Now much organizational analysis is not concerned with leadership in any dynamic sense. Its business is to show where authority resides, not moral authority, but the formal authority which commits a group to decisions. It is not concerned with who does the thinking ; it is concerned with who does the deciding. And the height of its achievement is to trace a mechanism in which the decision-making point is clear at every level. And so all well-organized institutions, be they political systems or government departments, industrial concerns, or hospitals, schools or armies or voluntary social agencies, have or should have their organization charts, showing who takes what decisions and where ultimate decision lies. And to that ultimate decisive element all other elements are subordinate.

This is good as far as it goes, but if analysis of responsibility stops at the level of organization charts, it misses the much more fundamental issue of how and why societies work and change or do not change and cease to work. Decision, as such, can be the exercise of blind or half-blind superiority. In relation to administrative system, all concerned may know where they stand, but that may not in the least correspond with where they want to be or intend to go. The despotic master of an economic enterprise and the conductor of an orchestra may appear to hold pretty much the same sort of status on an organization chart ; so may the " hands " and the musical performers. But, in fact, the relationships between the economic despot and his " hands " is very different from that between the autocratic conductor and his players, from whom he cannot extract more than he can inspire them freely to give him. The difference is between authoritarian superiority and inspired leadership. Leadership in industry as in every other sphere, is truly effective as inspiration grows and superiority diminishes. In political life, a government with a secure majority can either use its superior strength to dominate, or, without in any way relinquishing its responsibility, it can extract creative ideas from the opposition and from elements outside the narrowly political field. A sensitive government has an extraordinary knowledge of when to stop arguing and act and when to prolong the discussion in order to let thought and experience mature. Formal constitutional procedures throw remarkably little light on the actual processes whereby decisions are taken in healthy societies.

Nevertheless, in these formal constitutional procedures there is somewhere at the top a visible, identifiable, individual or body which carries all ultimate responsibilty, succeed or fail. And this supreme authority is created by human agency and can be shifted by human agency, albeit it may take a revolution, political or domestic, to do it. But among

Friends the pattern is somewhat different : " The power of God is the authority . . . of all . . . meetings " said the Yearly Meeting of 1676 and within the Society no individual or group holds responsibility except under God, in which situation all men have equal moral responsibility. The authority of God determines all human relationships and it is this conviction of the sovereignty of God, not as something to be fitted into the world of Cæsar, but as a constant challenge to it, that leads Friends at times deliberately and openly to become law-breakers and to regard Tribunals set up to sift men's consciences as of secondary significance. The sovereignty of God is understood really to mean something for daily living. That sounds well, but only those who have ever borne administrative responsibility in an executive organization of Quaker consciences can have any idea how difficult it is to find the Will of God with enough constancy and confidence to provide administrative clarity. For in looking for clearly defined working relationships, we again run into the problems involved in equality—equality before God, where the Spirit blows where it lists. What is the position of the leader of a Quaker group which recognizes that the power of God is the only authority and that God not only may, but in a measure does, express himself through each individual ?

As William Charles Braithwaite points out, historically, the Society has lived through a variety of conditions. " The early Friends believed in leaders, but not in a system : the Friends of the second period in leaders and a system ; the Friends of a later period were content to have a system without leaders ; but the Separationists believed neither in leaders nor a system."*

The first condition can be defended in terms of genius with which we are not now concerned. The third and fourth point the way to death. We had best beware of them. The second needs examination.

In essence this condition is indicated by the traditional

* Spiritual Guidance in Quaker Experience, *Swarthmore Lecture*, 1909, p. 72.

pattern in our meetings for worship, where, in the deliberate rejection of a professional pastorate, our triennially appointed Elders do not, or should not, conceive themselves as being given a mandate to run the meeting while their appointment lasts. They are responsible for maintaining a system, in which in the living waiting of all the " leadings of the spirit " may find expression through an unconstrained range of human agents. " The primary duties of Elders are to seek for true discernment in respect to offerings in the ministry, and to be loving and faithful in the service of that discernment ; to be diligent in spiritual travail, and prayer for those on whom the ministry of the word devolves ; to sympathize with them in seasons of conflict and discouragement." (Church Government Ch. vii.) It is their business to see that the channels run free, to encourage the flow of living water from a wide variety of springs, not to be a pumping station themselves. And their true status comes not from the fact of their appointment by their fellows, but from their capacity continually to gather up the living " sense of the meeting " so that the Lord's power issues coherently. The status of the Clerk of a Meeting derives from the same principle. The clerk is an administrative officer whose business is " to watch for the growth of unity in the meeting and at a convenient time to submit a minute expressing what, in his judgment, is the united sense of the meeting on the matter at issue. If the minute . . . is accepted, it should be recorded as the decision of the meeting." (Church Government Ch. V.) In Quaker meetings, confidence in the clerk or chairman is not primarily in *his* judgment, but in his capacity to gather up the threads of divine leading as disclosed through others.

The appointed leader of a Quaker worshipping or deliberative group then, must have capacity to stand back, encouraging and allowing others to express their partial insights, within the limits of the sense of the meeting. At the same time he has to discourage individuals whose anxiety to assert themselves makes them insensitive to the temper of the gathering. He has to make coherent the meeting's own unformulated stirrings. This is done with more or less skill in every Quaker meeting—and very many other gatherings that have nothing to do with Friends.

But while we have plenty of reason to know that in prayerful waiting, the Will of God can be revealed, there is equally adequate reason for knowing that not every meeting for worship or business held after the manner of Friends will be successful. All too often we know perfectly well that we have done no more than preserve the system, and any results of our business considerations are the consequence of maintaining " good taste " and not of living experience. Mountains of systematic Quaker labour can produce very meagre mice ; many a self-conscious minute proves on analysis to be an erroneous platitude. What can happen in the treatment of the same subject is well illustrated in the comments made by three separate Quaker groups on the disastrous Irish famine which followed the failure of the potato harvest in the autumn of 1846. The first reference is from the Epistle of Dublin Yearly Meeting at the end of April, 1847. It refers to " the awful dispensation under which . . . this land is afflicted " and goes on

> " We rejoice that . . . the hearts of our dear friends have been open in no common measure to administer to the wants of the suffering poor. . . . In this engagement . . . there is especial need of a watchful care that our minds be not diverted by the multiplicity and weight of these concerns, from a due attention to the other claims of religious and social duty . . . . Let us beware of any elevation of mind, arising from a consciousness of being made instrumental of good to others. . . . The labours . . . have brought us much under public notice, and into intercourse with those of other religious professions, who are engaged in portions of the same work . . . it is surely incumbent on us, if brought into a conspicuous position, however unlooked for or undesired by ourselves, to be careful that the honour of our holy profession be not tarnished by a weak and inconsistent line of conduct."

The epistle goes on to warn Friends against accepting military protection of their property or " that which may be under their care." It gives thanks for the preservation of Friends.

> " But let us also remember that suffering in person and property is often the portion of the devoted followers of Christ, and we have

ground to trust that their constancy under such trials will not only be owned by their Divine Master, but may, under his blessing be made a powerful means of promoting the advancement and spreading of the truth."

There is a group of Friends facing a calamitous situation with true charity, a little concerned to maintain appearances in competition with other denominations, but ready to take their own special share of the suffering in the name of Jesus Christ.

London Yearly Meeting, three weeks later, must have had this Irish Epistle before them, but they do not seem to have profited by it. In the course of a prodigiously long Epistle about many things there occurs the following reference to the Irish Famine :

> "Within the last year, it has pleased the Almighty to visit the nation of Ireland with sore affliction. . . . We feel that it becomes us to speak of the dispensations of the Most High with reverence and fear. . . . His creatures standing in awe before Him trembling and, it may be, dumb with astonishment . . . desire to be instructed by that which we have seen and heard . . . it may be, that in the sufferings which he has permitted to befal some of his children, he designs not only to bless his chastening to their greatest benefit, both in this life and in that which is to come, but to sanctify it to those that are round about them. When the adversities of our neighbours, their poverty and distress have the effect of softening our hearts . . . they are made a means of good to us, and we are prepared to feel the force of the words ' It is more blessed to give than to receive.' "

Could a better example be found of smug insensibility ?

The third reference comes five years later, when the Irish Quaker relief committee presented their accounts and issued the very careful critical review of their own work, already referred to.

True, the report contains the sentence " The awful visitation with which it pleased Divine Providence to afflict our country, was doubtless intended in wisdom for our good." But the general tenor of the document suggests that this was said in conformity with contemporary convention, for as a whole the report is an inspiringly honest account of human failings and sympathetic intelligence. Its authors say that even though, as a relief committee they may be criticized for commenting on social and economic issues they cannot refrain from pointing out that while " pure religion and sound morality are the only solid basis for national happiness," yet the famine was very largely due to a thoroughly bad system of land-tenure and a deplorable lack of educational provision.*

Here are examples of honest charitable feeling, bogus pietism, and robust intellectual analysis in relation to the same incident. While the continual possibility and frequent fact of error when system is dominant is one side of the picture, the other is the continual possibility and intermittent fact of inspiration when there is a framework through which it can express itself. If we recognize our own weakness and know that the love and truth of God abide, we can face mistakes with a sense of being released from our own limitations instead of with a debilitating sense of humiliation which may prevent us from admitting mistakes at all. A capacity to revise views about the work of God and to admit human fallibility is one of the most important characteristics of vital Christian leadership.

But while the method of seeking Divine guidance is well-tried in worship and deliberation, we have much less experience of what it means in large-scale executive operations, where hundreds of decisions have to be taken daily over wide areas, where joint deliberation would be impossible even if it were desirable, and where some individuals must be in a position to give instructions to others. Is comparable leadership possible in such circumstances ?

In Quaker meetings the clerk who gathers together the threads of the deliberations does not necessarily know more about any of the matters under consideration than does anybody else. But in relief work it is the job of administrative staff, and of section, group, and team leaders, to know more about situations in general than can possibly be known by the rank and file. By virtue of their functions they are in a position to give a lead in any issue within their province ; and they ought to give a lead ; they are also in a position to give

* Op. cit., Introduction.

administrative instructions and must do so, if co-ordinated
action is to be pursued ; at the same time they are, as it were,
clerk of the meeting in relation to their working group and its
members, so that they have the responsibility of encouraging
others to make their own creative contribution ; and finally,
they have the task of acting as the channel between the group
and the outside world so far as group or outside policy is concerned. In an organization-chart sense, this responsibility is
not different from that of the chairman of a company who is
also its managing director. In fact, it is quite a different situation, because while the chairman and managing director has
absolute superiority within the limits of his appointment in
the company, the Quaker leader of a working group is subject,
by the very nature of the organization, to the authority of
God, which may be revealed through the inspiration of the
most administratively junior member of his team. This
means that the good Quaker leader, while not shirking his
responsibility for giving a lead in virtue of his more extensive
knowledge, must be very sensitive to any truer, even if less
broadly based insights that can be drawn from his team-
members. Acceptance of the truth from babes and sucklings
is difficult to handle both administratively and emotionally.
And to precisely the degree that the Quaker leader gives
freedom for the initiative to come from others, he potentially
weakens his own position as the issuer of instructions and the
calculable negotiator with the outside world.

This kind of leadership illustrates well the difference
between intellectual analysis and synthesis and waiting on the
will of God. It is much easier to think than it is to wait
faithfully in worship, especially when something appears to
need doing in a hurry. The administrator with a wide range
of information and experience before him may not have much
difficulty in thinking out a line of action which he is satisfied
will meet the situation. But if he lays it before the group
he may very well find that while it can stand up to intellectual
criticism it leaves those concerned uneasy because, in some
way or other, it fails to correspond with their sense of what is
truly fitting, a deep uneasiness which cannot be removed by

argument. Now Friends are not an unreasonable body for the most part, and if they manifest a real uneasiness about a proposal it is pretty clear that it cannot be proceeded with under that sense of united concern in the spirit which must underlie corporate Christian service. Intellectual apprehension of ascertainable factors must give way before the sense that the Lord has not spoken, for without a sense of being encompassed by a cloud of witnesses, the Quaker relief worker or group cannot feel that the concern of the Society is being truly followed.

Leadership in these circumstances means, in the phrase of Miss Follett, that " the leader controls the group not by dominating but by expressing it." But, of course, this can very easily mean that there is no leadership at all, that the spokesman or committee simply do what a group requires, without giving a strong enough lead, intellectually or morally or both, to the best instincts of their followers. This abdication of leadership did sometimes happen.

One last observation must be made about this question of leadership in executive Quaker work. The more conscious the Society becomes of what is done under a Quaker label, and the more the Society feels that it must have a close understanding of everything that goes on, the more difficult does it become for the robust character or group with initiative to push out into the unknown and make new discoveries with the backing of the Society. W. C. Braithwaite, in commenting on early Quaker history, has a singularly appropriate passage, " The natural result [of the establishment of Monthly Meetings in the 1660's] was not merely to co-ordinate the discernment of the community with the spiritual leadings of the individuals, but to enlarge continuously, by the successive encroachments with which a system of organization aggrandises itself, the area of conduct over which the community exerted absolute sway. The spiritual responsiveness, which had been the glory and the peril of the first age of Quakerism, slowly died down, and a conformity to the authority of the community tended to take its place. Unity with the practice of Friends more and more displaced the older and more vital fellowship in the truth."*

Penn, Woolman, Elizabeth Fry, all rendered service which Friends are proud to claim as their heritage. I doubt whether any of them would have been easily sponsored by a modern Quaker Committee. In our day, the Friends Ambulance Unit was built on characters who either did find, or would have found it difficult to work through channels leading directly back to the " sense " of Yearly Meeting. Yet much of their service will prove to be a heritage that will be highly valued in time to come.

This brings us back to the earlier point about the conservatism of successful groups. In so far as success leads to self-conscious protection of a good name honourably won, it leads to orthodoxy. Quaker orthodoxy has tended to stress group unity. This is immensely valuable for it enables the well-meaning and the moderately able, to combine for service that is much better in quality than could be rendered by average Friends on their own or in non-Quaker groups. And within this sphere of official Quaker organization, leadership is a nerve-racking but not uninteresting exercise in socio-spiritual weather reading.

But I am not convinced that this is all that the Society can do for the world. I believe that while this kind of united group sense is a very great achievement, we should not be content until we are quite sure that if individuals like Fox, or Penn, or Woolman, or Elizabeth Fry, or John Bright, were thrown up by our Society to-day, they could be wished God-speed, even if their work did take them into some committee preserve, where their vision might be disrupting. In group terms, it is not good enough simply to be negative in relation to such an off-shoot as the Friends Ambulance Unit. With whatever aspects of its work and administration we may not have unity, its service bears authentic marks of the living Quaker tradition and we should be sure enough of ourselves to acknowledge spiritual community. It is a good sign that the Society is moving in that direction.

* Op. cit., pp. 66-67.

EFFICIENCY AND DISCIPLINE

In the preceding pages I have tried to show that while competent organization was necessary for effective relief work, the basis of that organization was not the authority of individuals or even of committees, but the concern of individuals and groups to serve under the authority of God, who reveals his purposes in many ways and through all human lives, in a measure. The splendour of this basis is the vitality that it can release, though the system through which it is released sometimes chokes it ; then there is danger in the stagnation or chaos that may develop if divine-human and inter-human relationships (to use the terms of Howard Brinton) are not faithfully and sensitively tended.

In so far as the bond between members of a socio-economic organization is a contract, efficiency and discipline are formally maintained, if at all, by the application of sanctions based on pay and status. Certain people have defined rights to give orders in the interests of the organization ; disobedience to these orders or neglect of directions given from above are punishable. In fact, it is a very bad organization in which efficiency and discipline depend primarily on sanctions of this sort. In proportion as organizations are well designed and managed, efficiency and discipline are functions of acceptable purposes loyally pursued.

Efficiency is sometimes spoken of as if it were something existing in its own right to be achieved by sacking 20 per cent. of the staff, cutting down the circulation of duplicated material by 35 per cent., and drawing up an organization chart. True efficiency is, of course, nothing of the sort. It is the result of good planning and good execution, so that the end product is achieved with the least expenditure of laborious effort—or alternatively that the outlay of much effort results in a correspondingly rich result. Efficiency begins with the clear definition of the ends to be achieved and finishes with the free and constructive pursuit of those ends by all concerned. "Free" and "constructive" are important. Where these qualities are present, the need for sanctions is small. People want to achieve the ends, and they will use their wits either to save effort, or, with the same effort, to reach better ends. Where they do not understand precisely what is happening their loyalty to leadership secures their active participation in change. Efficiency implies a readiness to change when it is sensible to do so. Efficiency in fact is a by-product of intelligent co-operation ; where this exists, so will efficiency.

Discipline is much the same ; where people have voluntarily committed themselves to pursuit of some common purpose and where both the ways in which that purpose is pursued and the development of the purpose itself are matters of general agreement, there will be general loyalty to what is personally required of the participants just in so far as the whole atmosphere of the organization is one of intelligent co-operation. Like efficiency, discipline is a by-product of human relationships.

In most socio-economic organizations, social and economic sanctions exist side by side with the general structural influences contributing to efficiency and discipline. In some, when the general atmosphere of intelligent co-operation is low, authoritarian sanctions are prominent, and the infliction of them tends to a still further degradation of voluntary responsibility. In healthy societies large and small, authoritarian sanctions are hardly noticeable.

In Friends Relief Service we had no sanction save one—the termination of membership. As mentioned earlier, we could not promote, demote, increase or decrease pay, or transfer between pleasant and unpleasant jobs. All these were contrary to the principle of serving " under concern." The Service was, therefore, entirely dependent on what could be done through intelligent co-operation. This is the ideal which many of us have for long advocated as the basis for more and more of our industrial, social, national and international life. Some of us still advocate it, but in the light of our experience in Friends Relief Service, we realize more fully than we did what a difficult thing it is to achieve and how much skill and conviction is necessary among those who practice it, in either senior or junior capacity.

In the field of efficiency our main difficulty was not slackness, though we sometimes ran into it : our troubles lay partly in straight human stupidity, partly in our inexperience, with most of our members doing jobs for which they had no previous training, partly in the failure of some of our members, with little previous organized work experience, to realize the importance of administrative continuity and coherence, partly in the difficulty professionally trained people had in realizing that professional relationships were by no means always relevant in an emergency organization of amateurs serving under concern, where departmentalism was tempered by equal moral responsibility for what was intended and done as a whole. I think it is fair to say that in all these respects F.R.S. was an organization capable of learning and that at times it achieved a fair measure of efficiency. But there was always a two-fold danger ; either that efficiency as an institution in its own right would be pushed so far by those with administrative authority that relationships became brittle, because they were no longer based on mutual obligations arising from a sense of fellowship ; or that " a sense of concern " and a knowledge of local needs and possibilities in the field were elevated to such importance as to justify abandonment by individuals of the principles of good order. Where these two dangers arose simultaneously, as they sometimes did, each was liable to accentuate the other, and if efforts at reconciliation failed there could be no alternative but some redeployment of personnel, usually a painful process, like surgery.

To the extent that these breakdowns were tackled with radical courage in F.R.S., it should be pointed out that radical action is easier in an organization whose whole basis is relatively temporary ; nonetheless, I believe it was also partly due to the sense of obligation to be loyal to the job itself, which pervaded the whole service, and was a natural outcome of undertaking work under concern. May the point be put this way, in all humility ? Friends' relief work has been happily free from the scandal of gross inefficiency. This has not been because scandal has been successfully hushed up, but because there has been an effort to spot inefficiency and to handle it at a relatively early stage with the painful directness possible in an organization with a widespread sense of obligation to God, and therefore to fellow-workers. But let there be no complacency. To " speak the Truth in Love " is difficult and disagreeable, and can easily be avoided by the common process of rationalization.

The problem of discipline is the problem of maintaining the best possible standards of detailed personal response in relation to that to which individuals are committed in principle. In F.R.S. good discipline involved two sorts of response on the administrative level ; on the one hand, there had to be readiness to accept instructions from those entitled to give them, without raising issues of principle demanding reference to the " sense of the meeting " at inappropriate times ; on the other, there had to be maintenance of personal standards of punctuality, tidiness, good manners, reliability and so on. About the latter, I propose to say very little. Our problem was the same as that of any other organization. These things are maintained very largly in proportion to the general quality of morale in the organization, reinforced by an appropriate word in season. Sometimes personal weakness in some of these respects is more than counterbalanced by the gifts of genius in other respects. At times more *spit and polish* would have been desirable, but had such outward appearances been purchasable only at the price of a formalizing of personal relationships within the Service, the cost would have been excessive. Suffice it to say, that we were not as successful as we should like to have been.

To secure the acceptance of instructions was much more complicated though the extent of the difficulty must not be exaggerated. Anarchy was occasionally approached, and it was sometimes avoided only by prodigiously hard work that could well have been applied in other directions. But we did not live in a constant crisis of discipline. For the most part, functional administrative instructions were readily accepted, because they made sense. But as we have seen again and again, any administrative matter may turn into a moral issue, involving principle, and in our sort of organization this tension between the administrative sphere and the moral sphere was always potentially present.

A. is engaged on a shelter project in a target area. Those responsible for the allocation of duties decide that his help is even more urgently needed to deal with a crisis in the running of a country evacuation centre a hundred miles away— and he receives instructions to hand over to B. and get to the hostel as quickly as possible. But A. may say that this will not do ; he has a " concern " to stay where he is. He feels as sure that that is the place for him as he was sure of his pacifist convictions when he appeared before his tribunal as a conscientious objector. And before anybody realizes what has happened, he has asserted a conscientious objection to being moved. Now this is difficult. In practice, nothing is more unsatisfactory than to send an unwilling man to join a small group on an isolated relief project. There is no reason to suppose that he will not perform his technical duties to the best of his ability ; but good relief work depends at least as much on conviction about its rightness for the relief worker as on technical abilities. And secondly, if a conscientious objector in an organization, the majority of whose members are conscientious objectors, and whose very existence is rooted in the conviction that conscience cannot be judged by man, claims a conscience on a matter, who is to say him " nay " ?

In relation to anybody unshakably claiming a conscience there were really only two possible cources of action—either the Service had to accept it ; or it could say, with more or less regret, that if the conscience were indeed inflexible on this issue, then there was no room for it in the organization whose ends were incompatible with that particular conscience, and the individual must therefore leave the Service. This second course coincides with that taken by some employing bodies, who do not question their employees' consciences, but who say that there is no room for such consciences in their concern—a perfectly reasonable point of view, but not always obviously so to the pacifist who is sensitive to " victimization."

Because in a matter of true conscience there can be no half-way between complete acceptance and complete break, it was of the greatest consequence that nobody in F.R.S. should raise conscientious claims when something less ultimate was at stake. To the credit of most members of F.R.S. a real impasse was very rarely reached. But it took much self-discipline to differentiate between rational preference and conscience—to see that disapproval of another man's particular type of pacifism was not necessarily good conscientious ground for refusing to work with him ; that happiness in some particular working group was not a conscientious conviction that that group life must be preserved when its functional purpose was superseded ; that nearness to one's fiancée or attachment to a locality are good rational grounds, worthy of being taken into account, for wanting to be in one place rather than another, but do not constitute the basis of claims of conscience.

These issues of discipline, when they arose, could only be sorted out by a mutual consideration of the purpose of the Service and of its needs from all its members. How long such a sorting out would take, or on what a scale it would be necessary or how urgently a decision must be reached were points that differed from situation to situation. But that discipline, to be worth anything in the Service, must truly and ultimately be self-discipline, was essential. This eased disciplinary problems in one way, but made them more difficult in another. It may not be out of place to choose an example that can easily be misunderstood, but that may help Friends to realize how easily difficult situations can arise, and what severe calls on self-discipline can be made.

A generation or two ago, nobody could have come into close contact with the Society without realizing that there was a strong and active sense among its members that the taking or offering of alcoholic drinks was wrong, both corporately and individually. For a variety of reasons, this is less true to-day : Friends as a body are not indifferent on the subject ; but rightly or wrongly we talk about it relatively little as a major social evil and a good many Friends are not personal abstainers, though probably very few are regular partakers. Consequently, in preparing volunteers, Friends and non-Friends, to go abroad in the early post-war days, nothing was said about the consumption of alcohol ; neither did those volunteers unfamiliar with the general outlook of the Society gather that Friends had any special views. The subject simply did not occur to anybody concerned.

Once abroad, teams could, quite unreflectingly, find themselves taking a certain amount of alcohol for granted. Water might be none too good and alcoholic drinks of a light character were the obvious answer to those who had no over-riding objection, gastronomic or on principle. Service members were often guests of other voluntary society teams or of local army units, or in the homes of the people of the country concerned. In these places, hospitality would often run to the offer of drinks, and if an individual member of the Service was not personally a teetotaller, he or she might naturally accept. It was natural to return hospitality, and in most parts of Europe, alcoholic drinks were not at all expensive. To offer guests an alcohlic drink was often much easier than offering a lemon squash, and quite possibly cheaper. And remember, that most parts of Europe are very hot or very cold for a large part of the year, that in relief work there was much moving about, often under very hot or very cold, and always under exhausting conditions, and drinks of some sort—it was often tea—were a frequent necessity of the work, quite apart from their use for social purposes.

In short, one way or another, for good reasons or poor, a modest consumption of alcohol became a not unusual part of the life of some F.R.S. teams. Neither to drink when offered it elsewhere, nor to drink or offer it in the team's own quarters, would have been in many ways actually *difficult* and even more so to discontinue it when once the practice had been accepted.

The practice was not shared or probably approved by a majority whether themselves teetotallers or not. Particularly in Germany there was a strong feeling that it was incumbent on Quaker relief workers not to indulge in any wasteful habits, and especially in those habits under the influence of which a good many of the personal failures of the members of occupying armies took place. Moreover, every member represented the Society of Friends ; the relief worker really had no private life, and those who knew the Society best had no doubt that there would be uneasiness at home about even a modest amount of alcohol being consumed or offered on German premises temporarily Quaker.

It would have been easy for the Committee at home to have issued an instruction—" No alcohol to be consumed or offered by Quaker relief workers." And I have no doubt at all that members in the field would have accepted such a ruling loyally ; moreover it would have been quite easy to apply, and to explain to any hosts or visitors noticing a change in team customs. "Instructions from Friends House" is an easy formula for both accepting and transferring responsibility. But that would not have met the real situation. For the Society has itself no positive statement on this subject—as it has for instance on war. The references to alcohol in our Books of Discipline, are all in terms of recommendations and queries, based on the individual's social and religious responsibilities. Strong though these recommendations are, there is no prohibition. Acceptance of a ruling on a major matter, apart from conviction of the spirit is of no value. If the habit were to be changed, it had to be because teams in the field came to recognize that renunciation was laid upon them by being sharers in the " sense of the meeting "—and in this instance the corporate sense of the ungeographically-united Society of Friends and its Relief Service facing the obligation to testify to the power of reconciliation in defeated Germany. It was months before alcohol disappeared from the sideboards or the conversation of some teams, but disappear it eventually did, as an act of self-discipline.

GOD'S WORLD

" While we deliberate, He reigns ; when we decide wisely, He reigns ; when we decide foolishly, He reigns ; when we serve him in humble loyalty, He reigns ; when we rebel and seek to withhold our service He reigns—the Alpha and Omega, which is, and which was, and which is to come, the Almighty."— William Temple, Lambeth Conference, 1931.

Just as, in a Meeting for Worship those present are themselves, yet also more than themselves (not I but Christ) and less than themselves (speak, Lord, for thy servant heareth), and out of this active-passive state, with a great sensitivity to others present, there comes the deep religious experience in which we *know* that this is God's world, and that we are his children ; so in Quaker service, the same series of tensions determines action. Just as in a Meeting for Worship the scholar may expound beyond the measure of his understanding, so may the executive leader act beyond his authority from God ; just as in a Meeting for Worship there may be empty silence for the hour's gathering, so in action there may be the form of corporate work, carried on entirely by its own momentum ; just as in Meeting for Worship there are the continuously insensitive, the silly, the inquisitive, the noisy, the quiet, the figureheads, the servers ; so in executive action, there are the clumsy, those who lack judgment, those who always want to be somewhere else than where they are, those with more energy than sense, the silent doers, the spent force. Yet, out of this mass of human failings and spiritual weakness, there comes from time to time, the truly inspired and inspiring meeting, the meeting which sometimes seems poor to its regular attenders, but which touches off tinder in some visitor ; so out of the weakness and conflicting emotions and interests and temperaments of active workers, there can and sometimes did spring the vitality of truly creative action. What F.R.S. was trying to do, and in its limited way at times achieved, was to carry over into the fields of executive relief

73

action, of accountancy, of publicity, the kind of experience that individuals and groups have known in Christian-Quaker worship.

The making of policy and the carrying of it out in a thousand daily decisions in a hundred locations was weak when based on " compromise "—a bargain between non-coincident views, embodying a bit of each, a sort of H.C.F. Policy was truly made and carried out when those concerned came together, not in a spirit of accommodation to one another, but in a spirit of common responsibility before God. To paraphrase a comment of William Temple's it was not by contrivance and adjustment that we found ourselves able to work together. It was by coming closer to God that we came nearer to one another.

That most of the time we *did* contrive and adjust was a measure of our human fallibility. The representative Conference was the most creative gathering in F.R.S., precisely because there there was less contrivance and adjustment and more real worship, enriched by the quality of experience brought to the gathering by those present, than on any other corporate occasion. The Representative Conference was the Quaker counterpart of a Joint Production Committee. It was more creative than any of us, in our secular moments, ventured to hope.

Has the experience of Quaker administration any relevance to the wider world in which we live ? I believe it has. It is true that we worked on methods that, superficially at least, were unorthodox. Like others we believed in leadership, initiative, hard work, the importance of policy and administrative order. But we offered no incentives and imposed no sanctions, either economic or those based on status. We distrusted personal ambition or the man " who wanted to get on "* and we had doubts about the importance of security. We believed in economic equality and we worked on the conviction that each member bore equal moral responsibility

* General Eisenhower expresses a similar distrust in picking his team for the invasion of Europe. For his exceedingly interesting comments on leadership, see *Crusade in Europe, passim.*

for the whole of the work ; but there was no equality of administrative responsibility, no equality in the sense of one man, one vote, and therefore no voting and no elections. Leadership always failed when it approached a claim to authoritative superiority and yet, though most of the members of the Service would cheerfully have gone to gaol rather than deny their consciences, signs of anarchy were not frequent. We believed that through the life and teaching and spirit of Jesus, God gaves guidance about the way in which he means men to behave in daily life, and we tried to live in that spirit.

We pushed these methods further than most social groups, but in practice most people are far less swayed than they seem to suppose by such a doctrine as that of the economic man or the conviction that democracy consists in one man, one vote, and the rule of majorities ; and are far more swayed by the sort of principles that motivated us. No one consistently buys in the cheapest market or sells in the dearest, not even those who earn their living by buying and selling. Every housewife and every commercial firm is partly influenced by human relationships built up over years and does not easily desert an old friend. Lots of people earn less than they could because they care more for something else, maybe principles, maybe friends, maybe leisure. Millions of people give their time to the service of their fellows, and not only the rich to the poor, as Beveridge makes clear in his book *Voluntary Action*. Millions are clock-watchers, but millions are not. In ordinary daily life, most people, most of the time, are generous, not mean, confiding, not suspicious, co-operative, not domineering. It is only in self-conscious corporate life that we tend to assume the worst motives.

In the sphere of management and government, one man, one vote, and the rule of the majority are convenient, if superficial, ways of assessing the state of opinion ; but the number of corporate issues settled in this crude way as compared with those which are settled essentially by taking the sense of the meeting is infinitesimal. We all recognize that it is a bad committee that is continually taking votes, that it is a bad majority which votes down minority views automatically, that it is a bad minority which is unconstructive before decisions and unco-operative afterwards. The stalemate in the Security Council, which follows all the formal rules of orthodox democracy, is a plain example of the barrenness of votes and majorities as such. And the business concern or industrial management which is consistently ruthless soon finds itself at odds with the community.

Lively communal life with happy zestful citizens, able to agree and disagree without either excessive regimentation or excessive division, does not depend on the regulation of mutual relationship by electoral devices, social contracts or contracts of service. These things emphasize our separateness and are divisive at times of strain. Healthy social relationships spring out of the recognition that we simply do belong to one another. We are equal, not in our rights, insistence on which is always divisive, but in our mutual dependence, as a man's mates strike and lose wages because they think he has been unjustly treated, or a thirsty man gives his water to an enemy who he thinks needs it more. In his Gifford lectures, Emil Brunner maintains that France is in such difficulties politically and socially because of the turn her thinking took when she set out to pursue equality on the basis of a social contract between separate individuals, an intellectual basis which freed men from the tyranny of economic and political over-lords, but which also freed men from common dependence on God, and which is essentially disintegrating because the intellect, as such, knows nothing of moral equality.

If democracy is to be capable of preserving creative freedom alongside the provision of adequate and ordered material existence for all, it must accept the tension between the moral equality which is basic to freedom and the hierarchy which is basic to orderly and dependable social organization. In major issues it is a terribly difficult tension to accept, and Christianity has done badly when it has offered men a prospect of escape from tension.

In the preface to *St. Joan*, Shaw writes of " a costly but noble state of tension " and goes on to say that " we must accept the tension and maintain it nobly without being tempted to burn the thread." With a three-hundred-year-old Quaker tradition of effort to accept this tension from a background of expectant worship, it was yet a difficult thing for us to handle in the Friends Relief Service. It is a much more difficult thing for a non-Christian world to accept in principle.

Yet throughout the world, and very specially in those parts which share the tradition of Christianity, there are millions of men and women who do, in fact, accept and maintain this tension in wider or narrower fields, probably quite unconsciously and with no idea of its ultimate significance. Wherever there are growing pains within the loyalty and harmony of the family circle, wherever there is mutual respect and a regard for sensitive human relationships between those engaged in industrial and commercial concerns, wherever there are committees, councils and governing bodies more concerned to do what is right than to minister merely to the glory of some person or party, wherever there are schools designed to help children to think for themselves rather than to accept uncritically the standards of contemporary society, wherever there is organized service by citizens for the welfare of others—in all these fields of sweaty endeavour and in many others the tension is being accepted and maintained, even if often only in very elementary forms. Wherever outward superiority is pressed and mutual responsibility is weak, there the tension is being broken by those who lack the courage and faith to maintain it and who therefore seek refuge from responsibility in power. This must be the end of all those societies, some wide, some narrow, which, failing to accept the dependence of all creation upon God, regard the processes of pure reason and of natural science as valid in themselves, apart from their inestimable value as ways of revealing God's world. Those of us who live within the Christian tradition, and more especially those of us who live in the English-speaking world, have a heritage of mutual responsibility which is still strong and very pervasive because of the quality that, for all its perversions at different times and places, Christianity has given to our civilization. As we repudiate the Christianity so shall we find the sense of mutual responsibility withering at the root even if it appears to grow in organized form.   And let us frankly recognize that Christian churches can be the most devastating enemies of the Christian Gospel when their institutional interests exceed their qualities of inspired leadership.   It is our business as Christians to recognize afresh and to help our non-Christian fellow-citizens to realize the origins of our own best selves.   It is our business to help forward in every way conscientiously possible the organized forms of mutual responsibility demanded by a society which knows as much about exploiting the possibilities of natural science as ours does ; but it is our business to see that mutual responsibility, organized and unorganized, is rooted in a sense of dependence on God, which alone can save the strong from the sin of exploiting the weak and which alone can give both strong and weak that peace which the world cannot give.

www.ingramcontent.com/pod-product-compliance
Lightning Source LLC
Chambersburg PA
CBHW031218270326
41931CB00006B/606